CHRISTIAN FREEDOM

If Christians conform to society's norms, it can restrict righteous freedom and hinder personal growth.

DOCTOR JOCEPHUS BINGHAM SR.

CHRISTIAN FREEDOM

No matter how hard somebody tries, they cannot restrain the freedom of my righteousness.

DOCTOR JOCEPHUS BINGHAM SR.

Copyright © 2023 Jocephus Bingham Sr.

Email: Joebingham3@gmail.com
Twitter @joe_bingha

All rights reserved. No part of this book may be reproduced, stored, or transmitted by any means—whether auditory, graphic, mechanical, or electronic—without written permission of both publisher and author, except in the case of brief excerpts used in critical articles and reviews. Unauthorized reproduction of any part of this work is illegal and is punishable by law.

Unless otherwise specified in quotes, all Scripture quotations come from the NIV®, the New International Version® of the Holy Bible. Copyright ©1973, 1978, 1984, 2011 by Biblica, Inc. ™ used by permission of Zondervan reserved all rights worldwide. www.zondervan.com. The International Version trademarks registered in the United States Patent and Trademark Office by Biblica, Inc

For Motivational Preaching And Teaching, Call 1-321-525-0327
See other books by Doctor Joe Cephus Bingham: Website: https://www.drbinghambooks.com/

ISBN: 979-8-89031-809-1 (sc)
ISBN: 979-8-89031-810-7 (hc)
ISBN: 979-8-89031-811-4 (e)

Because of the dynamic nature of the Internet, any web addresses or links contained in this book may have changed since publication and may no longer be valid. The views expressed in this work are solely those of the author and do not necessarily reflect the views of the publisher, and the publisher hereby disclaims any responsibility for them.

One Galleria Blvd., Suite 1900, Metairie, LA 70001
(504) 702-6708

CONTENTS

About the Author 1

Introduction 3

Chapter 1 Freedom 7

Chapter 2 The Origin and Freedom of The Righteous Roads 15

Chapter 3 Beware of False Prophets 36

Chapter 4 The Grave Clothes of Enslavement 42

Chapter 5 Graven Images Hinders Freedom 47

Chapter 6 Resurrection Power Brings Freedom 51

Chapter 7 Choosing Grave Clothes Over Freedom 60

Chapter 8 Freedom in Christian Unity 67

Chapter 9 Freedom in Christian Election 80

ABOUT THE AUTHOR

Bishop and Dr. Bettye Bingham celebrated their fifty-five-wedding anniversary on September 13, 2023. They have three boys, fifteen grandchildren, and seven great-grandkids in that blessed union. He founded the Glad Tidings Christian Ministries and Seminaries in 1984; upon the Scripture, Hosea 4:6: "My people perish from lack of knowledge."

Doctor Bingham's training manuals, journals, and books support Biblical Teaching. He is a published author and a renowned gospel singer. His purpose is to impart practical theology. He has prepared thousands of pastors and laypeople for the work of the Ministry. The LORD aided in establishing various faith-based educational institutes worldwide.

Doctor Bingham finished his formal Education in the Saints Louis Public School system. He completed his Undergraduate and Graduate studies at the Living Word College and Seminary, earning his Ph.D. in Christian Psychology.

INTRODUCTION

Secular lawmakers should not restrain or suppress Christian communication. Ancient Athens gave free citizens the right to speak, debate, and vote.

In the United States, their culture has attempted to imitate the specific laws of the Greeks. The First Amendment guarantees all citizens the right to free worship regardless of race, color, or social standing. Freedom of speech and the right to worship are part of the Bill of Rights adopted on December 15, 1971. Freedom, however, allows the Government to combat domestic or foreign immorality.

Every dictator culture has consequences for breaking its secular law. But as with all contemporary democracies. Wicked people use freedom of speech to incite hatred, which leads to violence and a deep-seated aversion that leads to racism.

However, the Saints share facts to persuade people to consider their faith perspective. But no one should employ violence to effect change. Non-aggressiveness will usually get us to where we want to be to see a righteous difference in sinners. So, repay no one evil speaking with evil. (Romans 12:17-21).

God intended for all His creation to grow and be free. Regardless, Satan's explicit purpose is to stop the progress of the Lord's people from realizing their power as ethical, free agents. So, Christians need to be aggressive in discipleship. Otherwise, their divine desires get overshadowed by fleshly cravings. Yes, Christian freedom is natural, but without supernatural discretion, abnormalities occur.

Notice how the Apostle John describes three elements that can obstruct a Christian's freedom. (1) "Do not love the world, (2) Nor the things in the world. (3) If anyone loves the world, the love of the Father is not in him, 1 John 2: 15-16. Faithful followers must practice their beliefs without fear of being jailed.

To illustrate, the writer has traveled abroad to countries where discussing the Holy Bible was unlawful for anybody. He is thankful to the United States; they added the First Amendment to the Bill of Rights, foremost to the Constitution. Gospel freedom includes peaceful assemblies, self-expression, and the right to petition the Government.

However, the issue with Christian liberation is that believers often take advantage of them. So, as communication becomes more efficient, accessible, and inexpensive, it allows us to use it for unrighteous purposes. Telecommunications technology can erode our freedom of expression without us realizing it. Sadly, we neglect the Gospel when we focus on this information technology.

For instance, instead of sending out bulk emails to spread gossip, we should pray when someone throws the Saints into a frenzy. But we usually use technology to tweet a reply or send out unauthorized photos, blog, and air out someone's mistakes. This spur-of-the-moment approach to spouting our abstractions has created a culture of criticism. We must be mindful of the consequences of relying on technology to lower someone in character.

Pray and do something positive about your assumptions before going into an outburst of rave. Yes, Christianity forecasts freedom in the United States of America, and social media makes it more attainable.

Therefore, it is more unchallenging than ever to abuse one's sanctification. Those who follow Christianity can be a source of transformation in the world. But they must understand their righteousness because of the Lord's mercy and grace, not their cognitive insight.

Freedom

Fighting for freedom can be a personal and complicated decision, even if it means risking one's life. Those who support this view highlight personal freedom and pursuing individual values. They argue that being a prisoner indefinitely can lead to a loss of dignity, personal agency, and the ability to shape one's own future.

Chapter 1

FREEDOM

The concept of freedom intertwines with ethical considerations. The writer will discuss the limits of freedom and the balance between individual rights and the common good.

So, if the Son sets you free, you will be free (John 8: 36 NIV84).

The quest for humanity's deliverance is the theme of the Holy Bible. But in only three chapters in the Book of Genesis, Adam and Eve surrendered their mortal independence by rebelling against the Maker of Heaven and Earth. To any extent, Jehovah needs His followers to survive impartiality by His Words; that was why He handed over the Ten Commandments to the Children of Israel (Exodus chapter 20).

So, if anyone imagines their prejudiced conceptions of human freedom are more rightful than adhering to the Holy Writ. Then, your self-promotion pride is a contributing influence. The Bible tells us, "There is a way that seems right unto a man, but the end thereof is the ways of death." (Proverbs 16: 25). Paul said, "Everything is permissible, but not everything is beneficial." "Everything is lawful for me, but nothing will have a head over me," 1 Corinthians 6: 12.

Further, there are no reasonable incentives for the Saints not to obey THE FIRST CAUSE. Their long-term bondage of rebellion has been a physical and Divine deficit for humankind. Opposing Holy instruction's initiative-taking effect invariably leads to ethereal depreciation. For instance, we can see the evidence in our original parents' sedition against the King of Glory.

Ignoring The Deity's Writ will affect one's faith when they brush aside—the Hope of Glory Commandments. The consequence is the relinquishment of spiritual liberation. Like Jocephus (the writer), most now realize their spiritual identity and believe that God is eager to be discovered by them. Still, it is a journey of authentic spiritual discovery that starts right where they are. Specifically, humanity has been searching for a way back to the Alpha and Omega since the first parent sin.

Nearly all sinners at a significant point, like the author's sins, caught him off guard. His future self undoubtedly shocked him with the terrible things he had done. Doctor Bingham found himself surrounded by tears as he questioned his identity and the possibility of redemption of freedom. He found his answer in Psalm 32: God can forgive us. More than that, he will deliver us from evil. Our part is only to repent.

Fallacious Independence

Many non-disciples and most Christians today squander precious hours adhering to the world's ideas of freedom rather than the Word of God. They think that if they attend Church regularly and make generous contributions, the Messiah must be pleased and grant their requests.

They have strayed from Holiness and are now in psychological captivity. Their thoughts were intensive in their exaggerated self-importance. Our Christian character erodes when we allow our ego to run rampant.

Note that conceitedness makes anyone believe and feel more significant and superior to everybody else. Arrogance hides insecurities and feelings of inferiority. A puffed-up innermost self wants ownership to control every circumstance and outcome.

If a Saint pursues a general division of temporal possessions, they honor religious objects, people, or entities besides the one true God. Usually, they are suspicious or blame others for their possessive temperament. Conceit is an exaggerated ego that leads to confined mortality.

Specifically, excessive greed can lead to a false reality, trapping the mind to want more. The only solution is to seek righteousness to remove those confinement imperfections. The unorthodox sense of justice and balance affected past predecessors. But within the Book of Leviticus, God gave Moses a set of laws intended for the Israelites to adhere to maintain righteousness. But the Gospel of the Christian faith states that Jesus brings us freedom from sin and grants us independence in this life and the next.

Holiness renews the spirit to a new intensity in our Sovereign of the Universe. Look, CHRIST, THE LORD, requires His people to meditate on His virtuousness. The devil's plan for humanity's existence is simple. He wants you to question God's Word by looking at your problems rather than the Supreme Being's. So, he attempts to make the wrong ideas more attractive to the human appetite to turn from Godliness.

The All-Powerful conclusive will is for Christians to advance HIS kingdom (Daniel 2: 44). The King of Glory's passion is to be in a loving interrelationship with HIS followers foremost and be free to practice engaging achievements. So, a relationship is the FATHER'S endowment; that being so, sainthood must be INTENTIONAL when the Glorified gives HIS grace away.

Righteous Liberation

True worshipers must honor and praise Jesus Christ with sincerity and truth. Seeing immature Christians give up faith because of spiritual responsibilities is disheartening. After a novice embraces dissatisfaction with righteous faith, they move on to add-on unhappiness. In anxious attachment, an upsetting emotion attacks the believers' integrity. Then Satan pursues unseasoned Christians to cause them further pain and distress.

Even though these Baby Saints' feelings or actions are not palpable, they remain mesmerized in the prison of a psychological fairytale. Untruthful thoughts bring them a fleeting nostalgia. Fear is their constant servitude, but they dare admit it with a dread of rejection. So, they abandon themselves in a vacuum of excruciating religious ambiguity.

Although vanity causes self-centeredness, they feel they can continue to do what they please. Immoral behavior enslaves a follower of Christ's perception.

Yet, at the worldliest, religion, separate from the Redeemer, is destitute of supernatural revelation or Godly guidance. Sinners and abundant carnal Christians focus on how their personage could lead to happy and functional behaviors. Without righteousness, humans are powerless to fight temptation. Faith in Christianity is essential.

Nonbelievers and agnostics believe humans can survive without divine intervention. True, they could have a worldly existence, not admitting that the First Cause exists, but their statements are empty of Devout experiences. Listen, presupposing that humanity lies in one's power separate from the Maker of Heaven and Earth is frightening. That means a watch may happen unescorted by a watchmaker or a story live without the storyteller or writer.

Even Now, pagans accept humans as neither intrinsically immoral nor innately righteous. Nontheists perceive the environment as sacred and humans as spiritually rich. So, they suggest that society has a fundamental nature like that of animals, trees, stones, and plants.

Taking an agnostic perspective, humans must take accountability for their ethical decisions. Skeptics still need to be convinced of the true nature of the Alpha and Omega or any spiritual matters. But human understanding is a subset of the Firstborn From the Dead Divine Attributes.

For example, the Apostle Paul was an essential leader of the original disciples. Pauline's Doctrines reality is the Deity of Word Made Flesh. He had faith in God's infinite wisdom and Omniscience. He was the second most influential figure in Christianity after Jesus.

The Church fathers traditionally attributed the twenty-seven books in the New Testament, 13 or 14, to Paul. He recognized the Gospel was for barring no one and that no barriers should hinder multiculturalism.

The Apostle's goal was to bring salvation through faith in Jesus Christ's redemptive teachings. Paul professes (Jesus) The Hope of Glory created paradise and all the stars and oceans, granting each nation the freedom of democracy. The All-Powerful Be the Glory Forever is an excellent summary of Paul's theology.

God's Freedom Through Nature

The environment does not pretend to be a piece that matters; it is not. There is no conviction in the natural surroundings, just a perfect picture of the creation of the Creator's sovereignty. Paul explained the Almighty showed his mercy through the rain from heaven and the fruitful seasons that brought food and joy to everyone, according to Acts 14: 15-17.

Though Mother Earth is only one of the countless ways, The Creator has laid bare Himself to humanity. Since the world's formation, the First Cause's invisible attributes have been visible. They can understand them by the things made, even His eternal power and Godhead, without excuse. See Romans 1: 20.

Still, professors of pagans and modern technologists try to answer questions about the purpose of creation. But their most searching issues are: Why does the universe live, and why is there something instead of not ought? Please understand it is uncomplicated for anybody to say God does not exist, yet not one thread of evidence substantiates their claim. The physical world, with its plants, animals, and environment, proves Jehovah's reality.

The writer, for example, can attest that God's Existence is nonfictional. He is enthusiastic and has taken his brokenness often, turning it into healing. The King of Glory takes what we lost and guides us to the rightful place in the Father. His friendship satisfied the writer's weariness and brought light to his darkness.

So, where could I go in the world from YOUR SPIRIT? Or where shall I flee from YOUR presence? "If I ascend to heaven, YOU are there! If I make my bed in Sheol, YOU are there!" Psalm 139: 7-8.

Psalm 8: 3 is the sacred songwriter's declaration of praise for God's created masterpiece. Simultaneously, it surprised the Psalmist that the Prince of Peace would give any thought to frail and limited humankind. But the Bible proclaims God's continual involvement in the ordinary world as the ONE who holds together and preserves all creations.

The Good Shepherd sustains and upholds all His creations, including air, water, soil, minerals, plants, and animals. Still, THE MESSIAH appointed humans to preserve the environment and wildlife. He charged us to care for His amenities so all living things can benefit from them now and beyond. And the King of Kings took the man

He had brought into being and placed him in the garden of Delight to cultivate and keep it. The First Book 2: 15.

"So, the Godhead formed humankind in His appearance. In the model of the Divine Being, He established them; male and female, He made them." Genesis 1: 27. Christians Stewardship believes humans have their creation in God's image, and He assigns them to manage the world.

In Psalm Chapter Eight, David compares the All-Knowing vast creation and the soul of humanity. The Everlasting influence on the natural world is apparent and should lead people to recognize Him. The Saints must never put their lives on hold, awaiting THE LORD'S passion while standing by for the environment to change. Christians are to generate an atmosphere of righteousness while living on Earth.

The environment inhabited by humanity is not a fabricated world created by humans. We inhale His air and drink His water; the sunlight sends light and warmth to the entire planet. But He gives the Saints the power to share His Gospel. He engages in the truth and encourages communion with everybody, regardless of denomination or ethnicity. Then, teach them that everything begins and ends with the Supreme Being.

> *"Beloved, let us LOVE one another: for LOVE is of Absolute Being; every one that LOVETH is born of the Holy Spirit and knows the King of Kings. He that LOVETH knoweth not the Omnipotent; for the Prime Mover is LOVE. The Creator showed us love by sending His only begotten Son into the world, so that we may live through Him."* 1 John 4: 7-9.

It is immoral and unreasonable for a Saint to use their influence to make someone feel insignificant. Leading them to believe they are not worthy of Christianity. It is the Christian vocation to let everyone know that the reverence of God brings liberation; however, sin holds a person in an unfair domain that quickly wears away their trust.

Jehovah the Father cultivates the human heart with his loving presence through nature's beauty in a fundamental process. God's Face shines on His people in the sun. His moon and stars remind them that THE LORD'S light and love glow to us even in the dark. Jehovah speaks to His followers and warms them from the heavens (Psalm 19: 1-6). The joy of the Redeemer comes to the righteous in splashing waves and playful animals! (Psalm 29: 3, 6)

In Galatians 5: 13-14, The Holy One condensed the Law into a straightforward directive for humanity to follow: "Love your neighbor as yourself." If humans repent and show their loyalty to others, they can live free of the restrictions of committing sins on Earth.

Chapter 2

THE ORIGIN AND FREEDOM OF THE RIGHTEOUS ROADS

The definition of the word (road) is a thoroughfare in the furthermost part of any place or point, with a specially prepared surface. Tradition has it that the birth of all roads started in the year 300 B.C. in the Roman Republic. Since then, humanity has depended on freeways for thousands of years to move and expand. When humankind joined to trade and do business, they connected themselves by footpaths and trim trails.

Even in this modern age, roadways are the most economical trip method. Societies use carriageways for multi-purpose Passovers, a wealth unacceptable and others acceptable. However, all thoroughfares are different. The majority are lengthy and meandering, with thousands restricted, rugged, and hazardous to traverse on foot. So, since no person is ever sure of any pavement condition, they should prepare for any eventuality of traveling.

Roadwork is vulnerable to hazards caused by unexpected events, restricted maneuverability, and construction apparatus. For instance, anybody who drives knows most roads are in better shape than others, especially if an area is under construction. More cars passing through worksites have led to increased accidents.

Interstate production laborers are in constant danger. Highway construction sites are the source of many work-related accidents. "The Bureau of Labor Statistics, in 2010, says 774 deaths at reworking sites, accounting for over 18 percent of all on-the-job fatalities that year."

The Road to Christianity

Christ-focused is not a safe expressway to travel. All other religions' worldviews share a common illogical flaw: (works-based). They cannot offer the unmerited act of kindness of the Alpha and Omega, the most enduring actions of Agape Love. But Christocentric is one of a kind, highlighting the feature of grace (the unmerited favor of salvation). Genuine confidence in The Maker of All Things increases believers' chances of ending up on a collision course with a non-Christian power. That makes THE LORD'S assignments the most dangerous belief imaginable.

So, when done right, there is a broad latitude to get into trouble with groups professing polytheistic religion. Ask fellow believers to pray for courage to overcome vulnerability and boldly speak the Word. In addition, we can prepare ourselves with the familiarity of the Almighty Word. Strategize both in the Gospel and disseminate ourselves in God's promises.

THE LORD is a source of mercy for those on the road to salvation. He gives people the freedom to choose, enabling them to make wise decisions in everyday life and act independently. Yet, we make thousands of choices without asking the Absolute Being whether we should do them. Misguided compassion can lead to an unfortunate outcome.

Still, everybody makes oversights that frustrate marriages, families, and businesses. Casting cares on THE LORD; anybody can rise above their inaccuracies. Mistakes are a part of life, but when we put them into the Master's Hands, He allows us to learn from them and grow.

But the antithesis of free will is as an infant sheltered from all harm and shut up under the stringent oversight of parents as a child. Then, at thirty, they left him without worldly experience. Could anybody call these guardians loving and merciful for treating a human like this? I pray our answer is no.

Therefore, as we travel on the road of faith, we should allow Jesus Christ to be our Chief Navigator as we forgive ourselves and understand our mistakes. So be courageous enough to accommodate blunders and let the lessons you learn from them help build a happy future. THE LORD created the Saints to be more than their miscalculations.

Traveling the Freedom Road

The King's Highway is more than a typical daily route for Christian travelers. Our Intercessor teaches the Saints are the salt of the earth and can still plan our method of travel, but it may not be the best approach. The Biblical example for following the Author of Life is much more Holy Ghost-led than contrived in human intention.

The King of Kings calls for Christians to plan, since they are only answerable for their results and achievement. So, stop blaming and do not make excuses. The Saints are who they are because of their own choices and thoughts they choose.

The primary goal of a Christ-centered life is to witness Our Lord with someone else. However, righteous preparation is necessary on the road to restoration. Acknowledging our individual experience of Jesus reduces emotional disruption. But the Saints and sinners have suggested that believers should not witness the Good News to the loss.

They believe people are good and that God will overlook their faults and give them credit for their favorable accomplishments on judgment day. Or the ridiculous reason: "Someone may ask a question I cannot answer." But boldly speak the word despite this and reply to them later with an answer you do not know. The Bible requests God's blessing on those who accept the Prince of Peace as their Savior. Salvation opens the door to enjoying a home in Heaven, a sinless body, and eternal life with Christ.

First, Peter 3: 15 tells us to prepare, which means organizing our thoughts ahead. There is an ideal moment to reply to someone's inquiry. But overly lengthy answers show a problem with the messenger message.

If you wait exceptionally long, you may have missed the opportunity, making them and yourself uncomfortable. So, when someone asks about your faith, seize the 5-second rule to acknowledge and give them the Scriptural reason for the hope in you. And always invariably observe Biblical principles when sharing the Gospel.

Ignoring Biblical theories disrupts the King's Highway in theological communication. Therefore, the Saints should constantly be impartial to the Paraclete of the Good Shepherd with any response to apostolic witness. It is why First Peter 3: 15 is the famous passage for the study of apologetics, which has nothing to do with apologizing but means: "to establish a defense like an attorney."

Jesus, preparing Nicodemus for life's Christianity expedition, said: The wind blows where it wills." Specifically, we should take the adage at heart: "Anything that can go amiss will malfunction. So, the Apostle Peter tells us, on the road to redemption, "Always prepare yourself to answer everyone who asks you to provide the reason for your hope."

The Saints ought to live a lifestyle of Christ, study the Scriptures, and pray for the Holy Spirit's guidance. Be susceptible to questions or opportunities to let your light shine so THE FATHER may get the Glory. Matthew 5: 16.

The Rough Road to Christianity

The author read about Christians' arduous pilgrimage during the Savior and His disciple's time on earth. Their struggles never shocked the writer that much. He brushed aside their belief constriction, justified by thoughts; "People did not accept a new faith movement back then."

But the death of Jesus was not the ultimate act. Ultimately, it was part of a Divine plan to save humanity from destruction. Central to the Christian faith is the belief that this one man died and rose again. Jesus' death enables Christians to heal their broken relationship with God. We know THE LORD'S sacrificial death as the Atonement. Or the reparation or expiation for humankind's sins.

So, the blessed and only Ruler of salvation message of Holiness for "All" threatened their traditional religion. Their central accusation against Jesus is His claim to be the King of the Jews. That eventually triggered the Ruler of God's Creation (Revelation 3: 14) arrest and crucifixion. (Mark 15: 2).

David's doctrine prioritized freedom, shaping Christian support for those facing financial inequality. The LORD preached social justice on the unrighteous street and challenged the status quo. For instance, an ancient Jewish sect was upset with THE LORD for not following their oppressive rules on the day of rest. In Matthew 12:1-8, the Pharisees objected to Christ's disciples eating grain on the Sabbath.

The Good Shepherd Messages offer eternal love, acceptance, forgiveness, grace, and mercy. But shocking is the observance of the traditional and written laws in this modern age. Christians still face arrests, abductions, beatings, rapes, torture, and killings because of their faith. So, the Horn of Salvation has never been a problem in society. He is the solution for a sinful, ill world, bearing EXCELLENT NEWS for everyone—no matter how messed up they are.

God founded Christianity on His gracious teachings through Christ. So, redemptive Holiness is not the issue. The righteous should focus on the value of love and kindness instead of blaming other beliefs.

Theological training aims to teach sinners and Saints that the Holy Spirit helps to achieve morality, with the Master at the center. But The Comforter has called the Saints to enlighten. Christian Education means to lead out of the darkness—a collapsed mind into the wisdom of the Infinite Paraclete.

Sin is driving the world toward destruction. Global conflicts are making poverty and homelessness worse. So, human brokenness is wrong with the logical order in this age. The Christian dream job is to become International Relations in righteousness. Matthew 28: 18-20.

But there is good news entangled on the mysterious highway of unrighteousness. Sometimes, the faithful may have to travel the dark road of despair, but the Glorified are never powerless. Despite oppressive policies, believers have the power to transform individuals through prayer. Then, the populace will change disastrous behavior.

For instance, the adage that prayer changes things is false; prayer advances people and resolves events. We can connect with the Divine through grace and supplication, shedding our ego and humbly sharing our hopes and needs. Talking with God is not magical thinking or a shopping list to meet our pleasure. It is not meditation but a direct address to God, communication of the human soul with THE CREATOR who created the human psyche.

Glorified Belief's freedom foundation teaches that all situations can help believers grow. Romans 8: 28. Divine meditation can lead people away from harmful cultural values. Promoting the Gospel should be a deliberate effort by The Saints, as it is beneficial to worship and be part of faith-based groups or discuss the Lord publicly.

The Bible tells the Glorified in Galatians 5: 1 that they are accessible in the Great High Priest: For liberation, "The Judge of the Living and Dead has made them free." Before the Hope of Glory died on the cross, God's people obeyed byway signs as an immoral compass to guide ethical lives.

According to Galatians 3: 19-24, the symbols were more meaningful in leading to salvation and true sovereignty than the Law pointers. Jesus Christ redeemed believers from the cycle of sin and death by sacrificing His life.

So, freedom is the absence of subjection to the Law of Moses and religious subjugation of denominational concepts. Being independent in THE LORD is the ability to worship whenever they want, without limitations or controls. But no one can understand the value of the direction of Holy democracy until they look back at the decaying turnpike of humanity and how they got their release.

Past ceremonies had rules and limitations for human involvement. The most egregious practices included animal killings and useless spiritual traditions. But freedom was through the shedding of Jesus' Blood in this age.

True believers must traverse the same path as those who mock them. Despite this, a child of God's journey has no recourse but to suck it up and turn the other cheek, Matthew 5: 38-40. Irrespective, apostolic preaching is imperative for a functioning, worshipping democracy. Yet, uncooperative comments from Christ's rejectors hurt.

No matter what others may say or do to counteract our efforts, we must persist in spreading the message of Jesus' love and glory. Christian travel starts with our desire to love and serve people as the Son of Righteousness did.

> *Regardless, in your hearts, honor Christ the Lord as Holy, always being prepared to defend anyone who asks you for a reason for the hope in you; yet do it with gentleness and respect (1 Peter 3: 15).*

Jehovah's Divine should relentlessly speak out against the chaotic crossroads of depravity. The Saints' spiritual conduct will suffer if they succumb to unrighteous influence. A stiff tongue about transgression holds the orthodox prisoner. So, the faithful walking on the freedom pavement of righteous understanding must share THE WORD.

The Glorified soul extends far beyond what humans can say or do with their pessimistic views. Proverbs 21:3 reminds us to show compassion and live consecrated to show our righteousness.

The Christian Bible continues to serve as a fundamental guide for ethical conduct. Therefore, believers should be careful when considering non-Christian religions. These are roads named (here and there) as it can cause the Saints to doubt their abilities. (See Proverbs 29:18)

The path of deceitfulness can impede the quest for sanctity by provoking consistent deviation from what is right. This results in a lack of awareness and readiness toward achieving one's objective. Christians actualize their life's voyage and selection through Alpha and Omega, as cited in Proverbs 3:5-6. Faith in Jesus is the sound approach to guarantee one's aspirations and deliverance, as stated in Ephesians 2:8-9.

The Saints recognize their redemptive direction to move toward their Holy purpose with the Redeemer. So, they withdraw from unrighteousness to a freeway that connects to a thruway of Holiness. Astronomically, humans cannot explain their overall survival journey.

However, the key defining trait of Christians is their unwavering belief in the Creator of the universe and his divine plan for life's journey.

Specifically, no person has crystal ball knowledge of where the years will take them. Without the Word Made Flesh, humankind uses three-dimensional metaphors to hypothesize time. The problem with their conjectures from culture to culture is that they disagree on right and wrong. They are in the hands of mortals to determine which allegories society should live by; hence, their human laws are only as good as someone's challenge.

In opposition, "The Ruler of Heaven and Earth determines the course of world events; He removes kings and sets others on the throne. He gives wisdom to the wise and knowledge to the scholars" (Daniel 2: 21).

No one can escape the bumpy expressway of unrighteousness. But the righteous must passionately trust the King of Glory and allow THE HOLY SPIRIT to take the wheel when driving on that busy turnpike of nonspiritual. Unwanted delays are still inevitable. Slowdowns may occur because of other aggressive driving, collisions, construction sites, weather, and halts.

Regardless, THE LORD'S promised, "For I know the objectives I have for you," declares THE LORD, "aims to prosper you and not harm you, deals to give you hope and a future." Jeremiah 29: 11. He is faithful! But it is not a mistake whenever THE MESSIAH pauses the disciples on Life's Thoroughfare. The First Cause is ready to teach His followers a unique journey strategy with great vigor. The Christian salvation highway leads to new experiences.

> *And I give eternal life to them, and they will never perish, and nobody can steal them from My grip. My Father, who has given them, is more significant than all; no one can pull them out of the Father's Hand, John 10: 28-29.*

The Necessity Of Forgiveness

However, the path toward the DIVINE and a believer's emotional emancipation is never a problem. It is the whereabouts of yielding to Holiness. After receiving Jesus, the totality of salvation teaches us valuable insights about our ultimate earthly fate. But the foremost business a Saint needs to do is seek forgiveness and repent of their transgressions for the slightest wrongs.

Penitence demands accepting responsibility for one's actions and showing repentance. Nehemiah 1:9 states that the "Supreme Being will gather the scattered from the remote heavens. And bring them to where I have caused My name to dwell. On the condition that you return to Me, observe My commands, and perform them."

I urge you to heed the Prophet's call to return to THE LORD, a fundamental plea of Jehovah's sovereignty throughout the Sanctified Bible. The Glorified first come to the Divine Father in repentance and faith, but contrition is not a one-time happening. A non-confinement of walking with the Omniscient is a continual atonement of sins. Atone is a Mosaic Law phrase representing a scapegoat for one's transgressions; see Leviticus chapter 16.

Again, THE LORD made no perfect person traveling on the King's Highway. But the New Testament Saints no longer slaughter innocent animals to redeem humankind's trespass. "The Son of Man came to save the lost." AND each somebody who makes a U-turn from sin to the Maker of Heaven and Earth in authentic contrition receives deliverance. Everyone will need amnesty, sinners and The Divine at an unspecified juncture. Forgiveness was the significance of the Holy One's life and sacrificial death on the cross.

So, *"Be kind to each other, forgiving everybody, just as the Infinite Spirit forgave you in Christ. Your heavenly Father will excuse you if you pardon others when they sin against you. Bear with each other and forgive one another if any of you have a grievance* *against someone." (*Ephesians 4: 32). Through the sacrifice of His Son on the cross, God provided a way for us to forgive our sins and find peace.

Freedom is for honest Christians. The Bible does not give the Glorified a license to do objectionable actions. Dishonest Saints cannot be accessible to Holiness if they have things to hide. Believers who cannot confess their sins are prisoners of their guilt. But repentance and Christ's love redeem them for eternity.

Godly parents do not cut off communication or ties with their children for making mistakes. For example, the progenitor's offspring may drive them furious or even heartbroken, but they still forgive them. No matter what, they are yet their lovable siblings. And Jehovah-Jireh does not stop believing in our salvation because we made a wrong turn here. Still, we must repent and continue the road of sanctification for a strong relationship with THE LORD.

Repentance is the freeway that strengthens the common lineage with their parents and the Good Shepherd. The children's dishonorable acts can alter the blood relation attitudes from justifiable to unsatisfactory. Parents should hold their children accountable for their mistakes.

Children often embrace immorality without considering their conscience. And this leads them to pursue sinful goals that cannot bring them Godly satisfaction. Then, they emerge as dishonest with themselves and others. So, when we allow sin to overtake an offspring's Godly Intimacy, fallacious illusions blind their sacredness.

Immorality corrupts, but sanctification fortifies morality. On life's thoroughfare of Holiness, the same is true of The Father's children as a parent's love for their babies. So, Adonai's Passion for us has not changed because of humankind's imperfect nature. But one's transgressive actions have other confining effects, both here and in time, without end. Therefore, asking THE LORD for forgiveness of sins is of prime importance.

Repentance and Forgiveness of Sin

Contrition transforms our minds to see things in God's way. But out of faithful repentance, the mind and heart about immorality change a person's behavior to honor God. Acts 26: 20.

Yet, self-condemnation can be empty when unhidden, then done in fear of THE LORD'S punishment (like Cain for the slaughter of his brother, Genesis chapter 4). "IF WE say: 'we have no sin,' we are deceiving ourselves, and the truth is not in us." The Apostle John declared this back in the first century.

Notice how he added himself in the statement ("we") 1 John 1: 8. John's accounts show we may still commit offenses. Usually, these will be inconsequential. Yet, a Christian can face serious problems when secondary transgressions are unrepented. Humankind is imperfect, and yielding to temptation is a trait passed down from our ancestors.

But even the most minor sins we discount the Saints should repent. Remember, all the tiny drops of water make up the ocean. So, miniature sins can amount to too much and overwhelm. Realizing the cost of our sins to the Lamb of Jehovah brings true repentance.

First Corinthians 15: 1-11 teaches that Christ's death, burial, and resurrection are the heart of the Gospel. So, rolling in the muck of guilt does not help to become pure. If we misbehave, repent, make what amends, atone for the wrong, and do better next time, see Proverbs 28:13.

But do not worry deeply about wrongdoings that make you unhappy. "My little children, I am writing these things to you so that you may not sin. But if anyone does acts of wickedness, the Saints have an advocate with the Father, Jesus Christ the Righteous, to ask absolution" (1 John 2: 1).

Further, The All-Merciful requires that the Glorified not tolerate wrongdoings in THE HOUSE OF PRAYER. Matthew 18: 15-20 explains how to address those straying from the path of righteousness. The congregation should put them out of the fellowship if they continue the road of misdeeds.

Though they may not be a part of the Local Church, their salvation is still safe. The Saints should pray and do all they can to return to a right relationship with God.

Transgressions hinder a Saint's communication with THE LORD, so they must set their unethical behavior right. "Your iniquities have separated you from the Almighty, and your sins have hidden His face from you" (Psalm 66: 18).

Repentance of contemptible actions is the only way to get that done. Still, no human can stop their sinning alone. They need to call on the Redeemer and request absolution. *"Yet now I am happy, not because I made you sorry, but because your sorrow led you to conversion. You became sorrowful as Yahweh intended and not harmed by us." 2 Corinthians 7: 9.*

It will be difficult for the carnally minded believer to turn the other cheek while speeding on the freeway of wrongdoing. For the taste of wickedness, they continue later transgression. But they do not want to face the repercussions of their wrongs. Sinful individuals cling to offense.

But there are consequences for those gifts of wickedness. People who suppress the truth in dishonesty will perish, as Romans 1:18 states that "the King of Kings' anger is from heaven against ungodliness."

Look, the passageway of compassion is the ingress and egress of powerful believers. The Alpha and Omega instructions are life-changing! We respect the Father's judgment by forgiving others and praying for our wrongdoers. Luke 11: 4 speaks of the Good Shepherd's advice to His disciples on the road to righteousness and spiritual freedom: "Forgive us as we forgive." Matthew 6: 12.

So, the compassion of forgiveness extinguishes toxic resentment; whether someone lied to or cheated on us by a companion, it is typical to become upset. But when we consider and acknowledge humankind's weakness, it becomes easier to excuse someone's mistakes and even our own. Only imbeciles wake up and decide they will do something wrong. Mature Christians do the best they can to follow righteousness.

If we claim to be without sin, we deceive ourselves, and the truth is not in us. (1 John 1: 8-9).

> *"Socrates explained many centuries ago that all people choose what they know will bring the greatest good or pleasure. But when they do not perceive accurately, they will accept the lesser interest by mistake."*

We know that situations and events are not always what they appear to be. Appearance can sometimes easily hoodwink us. So, this spontaneously leads to mistakes. Again, Jesus Christ showed his understanding of human fallibility when he said on the cross, "FORGIVE THEM, FATHER, FOR THEY UNDERSTAND NOT WHAT THEY DO."

Despite sinners and Saints, it concerns us whether we should forgive someone's wrongs, fearing a repeat of future conflicts. Just because you forgive someone does not mean you condone their actions or give them the right to damage you again. But it means you surrender all claims to retribution and vengeful feelings.

However, from the Biblical perspective, as Jesus was dying on the tree, He called out to God the Father: "Forgive them for they know not what they do." His statement did not take Him off the cross, but forgiving them releases Him from the pain of unforgiveness. Regardless of their forgiveness, there are still consequences HIS offenders must face. Ten reasons the Saint should repent:

1. It sets you free
2. It encourages you to push ahead with your way of life
3. It establishes your healing method
4. It eliminates the hatred and resentment from your spirit
5. You no longer allow the one who damaged you to rule over you.
6. You will have peace of mind
7. You have the authority to forgive
8. Amnesty is the toughest retribution yet the most rewarding
9. Compassion is the growth's most accomplished scholars
10. Mercy encourages us to discharge the sufferer's attitude

Prayer is a Must for Christian Freedom

Prayer has a profound theological connotation in every believer's thought-provoking obsecration. So, neglecting the plea of supplication and devotion is a soul-eating infection. Holy Communion is the essential duty of the Saint's accountability. Time with the Counselor brings righteous consequences.

Prayer is a way to express gratitude, praise God, ask forgiveness, and talk to Him like a friend. The mysticism of communing with God's Holiness is not complex or sophisticated.

So, one need not be eloquent in speech for it to work. But if someone fills the mind with unrighteousness, prayer can become a prison of false illusions. Not conforming to Holiness during prayer leads to hollowed tradition or simple laziness. Hackneyed phrases constantly create a misleading fantasy to hold the innate spirit captive in doubt. Use your dialog to talk with THE LORD, not the pastor's syntax or someone else's clichés.

Our devotions are insignificant and counterproductive to God trying to mimic others. When you talk to God directly and honestly, you can expose fake stories and witness His compassion towards the virtuous. False piety often results in dull, repeated spiritual phrases.

So, on the high road of conciliation, let Nehemiah's undeviating prayers serve as an example for the Christian nation; whether everything is falling apart or going well, call on Jesus consistently using simple language. Devotion to the Son of Righteousness is a common challenge for Christians. Especially when they believe they believe in walking on both the worldly and Divine paths.

But most struggles are too incomprehensible for humankind. We cannot rely on conventional weapons in this battle. We are not fighting against mere flesh and blood but against powerful spiritual forces of darkness (Ephesians 6:12). Paul stresses that the battle is not physical. So, the righteous do not face a natural enemy, but a non-material one. Prayer can help individuals reach their full potential and overcome discouraging challenges.

As challenging as Nehemiah's campaign was, the course will be rougher on this Christian journey, so give cumbersome concerns to the Prime Mover. For instance, Nehemiah was not a mere fortune-hunter; he knew even the roadway to rebuilding the wall of Jerusalem would be a challenge with an accumulation of complications. So, he took his burdens to the Maker of Heaven and Earth and requested His help.

Every believer who tries to hold on to problems misses Jehovah's exit to life's smooth transportation. Jesus Christ formed humans with a passion for seeking Him. So, asking Him for advice is not admitting failure but recognizing He is the King of Glory, the Creator, and the Master Builder. The LORD is near to everybody who appeals to Him, to anybody who calls to Him. Psalm 145: 18. For instance, HE brought Adam into being with a need for encouragement from Eve.

THE SON of RIGHTEOUSNESS fashioned the First Mother with a distinct purpose in mind: (compatibility) "Not good for man to be alone; I will make him a helper suitable for him" (Genesis 2: 18).

When expressing gratitude to the Almighty, God's family must remember that it is not enough merely to articulate words. But to live by those principles, they vowed during worship. So, growing into a better Christian, one should appreciate individuals who help prepare them for life's journey for who they are today.

When the King of Kings gives His people an assignment, He expects them to petition for His support. Nehemiah 1:11 suggests that THE LORD leads believers to self-determination and success. So, he kept his eyes and heart open to THE LORD'S graces through prayer.

Jesus said, "Whatever you seek in Immanuel's Name, so be it, to Glorify Jehovah through the Son." See John 14: 13-14. In comparison, the Sovereign of the Universe does not permit His Saints to request anything that comes to their minds. Their requests must exalt the Blessed and only Ruler. Foolishly believing the Creator must give us what we demand is unskillful in honesty.

Not seeking the SPIRIT OF TRUTH, the pure in heart restricts their freedom to act without Immaculate Guidance. They usually believe they are absolute, but they are on an accident-prone road, setting themselves up to crash. Unless individuals accept guidance from the Divine Being, they will fail. Successful individuals shape their destinies by seeking the Almighty and not shying away from demanding tasks. For instance, practice does not make perfect - what we do in practice makes perfect.

Proficient adherents of Christ set targets, formulate ethical decisions, and chart their path. They envision accomplishment and consistently increase in knowledge and study. If one does not follow the mentioned traits on their life journey, their trip will turn into a funeral plan conducted by Satan.

Then fear, anger, and failure make the evangelical journey impossible. In addition, quick-tempered Divine beings are typically hypersensitive about anything that makes them angry. These are primarily thin-skinned

Saints oversensitive to critique. Mature Christians usually have a good sense of humor and humility, so they do not take every little criticism seriously.

Holy prayer teaches communication with the Spirit of the Omnipotent. For instance, there is value in praying for those in need, people who cannot pray for themselves, and believers who need our strength and support. So, the All-Merciful left us an example of what the supplicant should do when facing adversity: take them to THE SAVIOR. But never put on a false front, shut down, break rank, or isolate yourself from those who can help. Run to Jesus!

James 5: 14-16 asks:

"Is anyone among you unwell?" "Call for the elders of the Church, and sanction them to offer prayers over them, anointing him with oil in the name of the Redeemer. And the invocation of their confidence will heal them. And if he has committed sins, the Savior forgives them. So, confess your transgressions and entreat one another so the Creator can restore both to Holiness."

On the road to salvation, praying for those souls who cannot pray for themselves is a work of art. Intercessory worship is the map that leads to the throne of righteousness. So, the inherent mission of Christians is uncomplicated to understand. Seeking the Mediator's help allows us to witness the Holy Ghost performing many righteous tasks.

A reverent petition made to THE HIGHEST for someone else produces strength and support on this sacred journey. Listen, *the pain affects the whole anatomy when the smallest finger hurts.* Likewise, the entire body is happy when an individual appreciates a person. At the heart's core, a prayerful plea of intercession intervenes in an urgent crisis on behalf of another; their prayers are a blessing to them.

"Whenever a parish member suffers, all constituents should share in their grief, and when someone converts, everyone joins in their joy." 1 Corinthians 12: 26.

So, whenever the saints join the thoroughfare of invocation, they realize the power of a virtuous person as they pray in Jesus' name. Prayer through faith provides believers with the answers to receive victory. So, trust in yourself, have commitment and dignity, and never abandon your goal; the price of success is excessive, but so are its incentives. The Messiah lives within the righteous, so only they can demoralize themselves. Do not let your troubles destroy you; pray instead.

Godly Sovereignty is the Saint's fundamental birthright. The Word identifies these rights explicitly throughout the Christian Bible. The Infant Redeemer's intervention is essential for establishing laws and principles.

Ask THE LORD for guidance and strength daily when they do not pray. The disciples of Christ are led astray by Satan's immoral persuasion. Then, they doubt their worthiness in the eyes of the Righteous Shepherd. The devil's mandate is to bring the Exalted into bondage again. But he cannot mislead them if believers reawaken themselves daily to who they are in Jesus through supplication.

Upright people should follow the King's Highway and take a page from Nehemiah's and the Patriarch's commitment to their prayer life. The Most-High people understood that their loss of Jewish self-government was a punishment for their sinful offenses. They persistently petitioned the Supreme Goodness of Glory to seek forgiveness and restore their former way of freedom.

Immoral actions left unrepentant are morally wrong acts against the King of Kings or His Divine Law. The LORD prepared a pathway of righteousness for believers to walk with Him faithfully.

Still, no human has a travel-free passageway in life. So, the righteous must repent of their trespass consistently. Repentance acknowledges transgression with a commitment to change. Consistent worship guides the Saints to nurture godliness by eradicating habits that lead to the road of sin.

For instance, the Scripture tells how the Prophet Nehemiah had a daily thoroughfare schedule for prayer for months relevant to the broken wall. So, when the hour was perfect, the man of Jehovah spoke to the emperor regarding the wall's issue. He received permission from the pagan King to rebuild with the building materials (2: 1-8).

The Christian faith journey will have downs and unforeseen turns. Believers may find themselves in a cycle of spiritual apathy, causing a loss of interest in the synoptic Gospels and prayer.

The Old Testament has a term for individuals who show no interest or feelings towards the Scriptures, known as "backsliding." This term refers to people who were once lively and enthusiastic about THE HOLY ONE but have allowed sin and procrastination to lead them astray.

Their faith weakens, and they stray from Christ instead of approaching Him. Usually, neglecting to read the Inspired Writings and deviating off the path of righteousness causes the saints not to focus on the Almighty. If a Saint has fallen off course with the King of Heaven, calling on Him is the best way to discover Him again.

The All-Merciful created humans who need to interchange with Him through prayerful passion. Praying is talking to the Incarnate Word, like friends speaking to each other, bringing them closer together through sharing. When the followers of HOLY and TRUE pray, they expose their innermost being on the thoroughfare of freedom with THE FATHER. Divine supplication refreshes their memory; they depend on the Bread of Life, not themselves. So, in devotion, Jesus Christ transforms His People and renews them as free moral beings.

But evil has an expressway speed of taking hold of a non-meditating Saint's heart. Then, rude habits make it challenging for them to separate themselves from the passageway of immorality. Sin forms a chain that only the Savior can break for carnal Christians. Mature Saints must worship to pray for weaker followers.

Humanity will blame shifts instead of taking responsibility for their immoral behavior. Or they spin inordinate activities, thinking in the circulation of theories that are not worth doing. Yet quoting and studying the Good Book is a significant way for anybody to manage and shed grave ideas about the world.

Adhering to THE WORD can transform emotions into more resolute actions, mainly if you are impervious to novel concepts. Still, the Scriptures are most effective in response to negative thoughts. Instead, we justify telling ourselves to escape by witnessing our testimony. The LORD is not a poky driver (slow) in keeping his promise, as humans understand slowness. Conversely, the Maker of Heaven and Earth is patient with us, not wanting anyone to perish but for everyone to travel the road of repentance (2 Peter 3: 9).

Chapter 3

BEWARE OF FALSE PROPHETS

The Two Categories of Fraudulent Prophets:

(1) In the Christian faith, a deceptive prophet erroneously alleges that they have a gift of divine foresight to speak for Jehovah. In a broader context, they allege a unique bond with His Divinity and establish themselves as a spiritual authority. They foolishly claimed they were an adept of the Holy Spirit, a revivalist, or a teacher in the likeness of Christ.

(2) These unscrupulous soothsayers are notorious for their capacity to dupe and sway others with their abilities. So, self-interest, greed, and personal "gain" usually motivate their fallacious appetite.

The Bible tells us to believe not every spirit but try the spirits, whether they are of Jehovah, because thousands of bogus forecasters go out into the world. There are two kinds of malevolent crystal gazers. (a) Individualistic ones outside the Church who do not inflict harm on believers. (b) Those who come to Church masquerade as benevolent individuals to deceive the devout for personal profit.

They both are prognosticators who bring a directive, not from God. Their communication contradicts God's instructions, often appealing to our earthly cravings or passions. That stated, believing either of the two can rob Christian freedom. The Redeemer said: "The Grape farmers gather their fruit apart from thorn bushes. You will know them by their fruits." Matthew 7:15-20. So, every good prophet bears a message that aligns with the Written Word.

Jesus warns disingenuous prophets are the greatest threat to Christianity's independence. Yet, it is a reprimand that most Saints may not consider after reading the Bible. Both secular and righteous convictions prioritize economic stability and social values. The two bullet points may have a momentary effect. However, most individuals consider spiritualists a catastrophe because of their current and future influence.

Those who believe a false apostle's story have put themselves under a liar, who may not even be aware of their falsehoods. Pernicious liars are compulsive hypocrites, and they are talented performers. Demon's possession is not conceivable by followers of Christ. But when true believers lend credence to chronic perjurers, they allow Satan a toehold in their redemptive life, limiting their freedom. The Bible commands us: "And do not give the devil a foothold" Ephesians 4: 27.

So, when unholy spirits persuade Christians, it becomes unfeasible for them to obey the HORN of SALVATION. When members doubt the Author and Perfecter of their Faith, they misinterpret the origin of ethical confidence. Belief in or acceptance of the Infinite Spirit does not imply assurance or result from absent indecision. The truehearted seer never uses prediction, sorcery, or astrology. See Deuteronomy 18: 9-14; Ezekiel 12: 24; Micah 3: 7. The authentic prophet never will alter the report to cater to the appetites of the population. Jeremiah 8: 11; 28: 8; Ezekiel 13: 10.

The writer of the Second Gospel explains that in the account of the Son of David healing a child possessed by devils, chapter 9: 14-27. The boy's father requested help in front of a crowd; religious leaders were inclusive. He told the Atoning Sacrifice of Our Sins that He had asked His disciples to cast the demons from the boy, but they could not do so. Then Christ said, verse nineteen, "Oh unbelieving generation, how long shall I put up with you? Bring the youngster to Me." Mark 9: 19.

Jesus healed the child. Case in point, true prophets always carry the Almighty's Nature within their innate spirit. Prognosticators filled with the Holy Spirit are true prophets. But money and self-interest motivate false prophets. Prophets of Jehovah, like their HEAVENLY PREDECESSOR, are no respecter of persons. They speak Jehovah's Message faithfully, uttering His Purpose, whether their audience may agree. Whatever is said or done, THE FATHER will support a recent, appropriate, timely expression of HIS HEART.

THE LORD encourages every Glorified to build on their belief in the Word. Believe in Jehovah-Nissi. *Therefore, I tell you, whatever you ask in prayer, believe that you have received it, and it is yours" (Mark 11: 22–24).*

The Mediator of the New Covenant encourages us to beware of false prophets, as stated in Matthew 7:15. Beware means being cautious and alert to dangers. Pastors must especially emphasize deceptive teaching and misleading teachers, whose ways are clever. These mendacious soothsayers have a mandate to steal Christian freedom. They clothe themselves with lamb's wool but are wolves.

Whether solid or weak conviction, it does not affect one's salvation. Satan and his mythical creatures have no claim on the Glorified. The Chief Cornerstone paid humankind's cost for their transgression by His Blood. Even though the righteous might obsess about doing the unethical and execute it. Still, sin does not subjugate their eternal, nor can they self-acknowledge as a dishonorable doer. The Great Shepheard does not call the qualified for His work. They are a dime a dozen. El-Shaddai calls the individuals devoted to His righteousness, equipping them for the tasks ahead.

A trespasser has the compulsion to do morally wrong and enjoys it. But a follower of the TRUE VINE may conduct an unlawful act, but they will repent. The canonized cannot enjoy immoral acts and encounter no remorse. Thus, no New Testament writers uphold spiritual constraint or a Saint committing unforgivable sin; they delineate the difference between supporters of Immanuel and unbelievers. The Apostle Paul explains the dissimilarity of the saved and the unsaved in all his Epistles, especially in Romans, chapter 8.

> *"You, however, the Paraclete, controls not by the sinful nature, but by the Spirit of Truth. The Holy Ghost of the Almighty dwells in you. But if anyone does not have the Comforter, he does not belong to the Lamb of the Omnipotent. But if The Redeemer is in you, your body is alive because of sin, yet your soul is conscious of righteousness. The power that raised Jesus from the dead is living in you."* Specifically, believers can be guilty of disobeying Jehovah, but they cannot practice disobedience. (1 John 3: 4–10).

A note: Nonexistence in the Bible tells of any Christian consumed by familiar spirits. But it clarifies that the followers of The Good Shepard are to refrain from unrighteousness by resisting the evil one. Christians are to exercise and teach resistance to the devil when it concerns them or another follower.

Jehovah's people are not in the business of casting out the demons of Christians. The Savior paid the cost of their righteousness with His Blood. (James 4: 7, 1 Peter 5: 8-9). Likewise, there is a distinction between a believer haunted by sadists or oppressed or influenced by them. However, people without Christ have no hope, nowhere to turn, and no future. Corruption leaves them vulnerable to demon possession.

For example, sinners devote themselves to the fallen angels' unrighteousness and enjoy it. Lucifer and his demons target a child spiritually to push sinful behavior. The Bible does not mention removing an unholy creature from a disciple (Ephesians 6: 10-18). Again, God has given them resistant power. And Jesus said, "Take heed; no one leads you astray (Mark 13:5–7, 13: 21–23). In addition, the person who lives by the flesh (without Christ) is now in bondage to demons, Romans 8: 5-13.

The Sacred Writ warns us that in times of violence, immorality, and anarchy spread while Holiness's love dwindles, 2 Timothy 3:1. Humanity will admire themselves, money, and unholy things. They will be unthankful, disobedient, unforgiving, and slandering. They will be traitors, headstrong, and pleasure seekers instead of lovers of God. So, as awful as the moral state of humans is, it may worsen in the coming years.

No verse in the New Testament suggests a date for Jesus's return. Seeking to predict the apocalypse might spiral into a form of spiritual persecution. Anticipating hell, judgment, or demonic activity influences us as we adopt a non-conformist attitude.

The Bible undoubtedly tells the Glorified to be vigilant. But the Expected Savior likewise explains that no one can tell that the Saints live in the apocalypse. Once more, Immanuel Himself repeatedly said that no person knows the day or the hour of His return (see Matthew 24: 36, Mark 13: 32, and Acts 1: 7). So, it is senseless and bondage for Christians to travel on the busy thoroughfare of apocalyptic paranoia. With eyes wide open, let us remember the calamities that have yet to happen.

Over the past few decades, people have predicted earth-smashing disasters; humanity is yet on the planet. Events are signs of the end: famines, earthquakes, floods, troubles, persecutions, destruction, and wars (Mark 13:7-9). But has there been a time in the world's history when catastrophes were not so? Still, not all of humankind's apocalyptic endings and predictions with due dates have come true.

Predicting the millennium is hard, but that does not stop false prophets from trying. Yet, their events are as unpredictable as when humans could not google one's inquisitiveness away. Society knows more about today, but tomorrow remains as mysterious as ever. The highway to humanity's end is coming! The Book of Revelations is the Christian eschatology guide that proves it. Disagreement is likely to arise from forecasting the future.

Chapter 4

THE GRAVE CLOTHES OF ENSLAVEMENT

Chapter eleven of the Apostle John tells of the first step to freedom. The story tells how the Author of Salvation adored Mary, Martha, and Lazarus. But the sister's brother became fatally unwell while Immanuel ministered out of town. When He got the news, the Judge of the Living and Dead stayed ministering twice as long. When He returns to Bethany, Martha vents her frustration and sorrow with her words.

Mary's sister was so upset about her brother's death that she did not realize her statement made her worry about the past. Her grief, worry, and disappointment prevented her from making a helpful decision about Jesus. Still, Martha's words are not of reproach, but one of regret. For instance, "Master, your friend may be here had you been in town. But I understand YOU have a widespread outreach ministry."

She understood doubting God's promise equals calling Him a liar. Bringing our pains to Jesus opens our eyes to more profound truths He wants the Saints to learn. The Alpha and Omega previously knew our hearts, and He knows our pain. Not only will He manage His people's misery, but He can also replace despair with hope.

Do not be harsh on Martha. Her faith is common among Christians who question God's ability when in trouble. She knew the Man from Heaven's competence to heal, turn water into wine, cast out evil spirits, and quiet storms. But this was a departure from life! She wonders if her emotions and desires were a human infatuation with deliverance.

Doubt has always been a problem with the Saints. Abraham's wife laughed when the Supreme Being promised her a child in her old age. The problem was that Sarah's amusement reflected her distrust in the ability of God's Omnipotence Powers. Unbelief is a more consequential sin than most Christians realize. Martha would learn what Sarah learned not through her sorrow but her chuckle, not anything Too Challenging For The Redeemer (Genesis 18: 9-15).

Unpleasant emotions can lead to questioning our beliefs. Martha thought, I'm aware of THE COMFORTER's work in the past, yet death is a challenge no one has overcome. In addition, from Martha's disbelief, miracles are okay; despite this, we are speaking of not the time for wonders. Martha thought nobody had ever returned from a "four-day breathless body." Her theology is correct, but she forgot what everybody fails during trials, that JEHOVAH-JIREH is right there, standing next to us to supply our needs.

The Man from Heaven kindly told her, Martha, I alone am the rebirth and the life. Then He asked her, "Do you believe." She responded, "Yes!" But she thought the Lamb of the OMNIPOTENT referred to the resurrection. After the Almighty visits His friend's secure tomb for four days, He orders them to move the stone that had sealed it. Not that Jesus cannot remove the boulder from the grave. THE SON of JEHOVAH can speak a Word, and the headstone must shift aside.

But human help with the burial mound only proves that each Saint has a role in proclaiming the Good News of His salvation. It's the privilege and responsibility of every Christian to glorify the Lord and share His Transformation News.

"I will give you a new heart and put a new spirit in you; I will remove your heart of stone and give you a heart of flesh." Ezekiel 36: 26 (NIV84). There is no higher calling in the Christian faith than ambassadors for the King of kings and taking His message to a lost and dying world.

JEHOVAH knows our lack and everything regarding our way of life. (see Matthew 6: 8). But because of His righteous constraints, He prevented Himself from intruding on humankind's independence. He calls for believers to intercede for His guidance in their affairs. The Good Shepard clarified Godly help when He shared with His disciples to request the "Father's will to be on earth, as in Heaven." (Luke 11: 2).

Immediately after they removed the stone and prayed at the burial ground, He called Lazarus (His dead friend) from his crypt. Likewise, Christians are to reach the sinfully lifeless to the living. Salvation is unquestionably possible for every sinner, but the Saints must ensure they do so out of genuine love and seriousness. Without exception, most followers of Jesus Christ want to fashion unsaved people.

Be careful in emphasizing misconduct. The flaws that one observes in others can often highlight their shortcomings. So, before a Saint withstands the worst of bringing a sinner's sin to their attention, be confident they have theirs' in check. In Matthew 7: 5 (NIV84), THE LORD rebuked the religious leaders with these words. "You hypocrite, first take the plank out of your eye, and then you will see clearly to remove the speck from your brother's eye."

The mummified resurrected body of Lazarus was a sight to witness! Then Jesus commanded the dead man to come forth, bound hand and foot with grave clothes and his face wrapped tightly with a napkin. He was alive but could go nowhere or help himself. A note: There is no hint in the Scripture that the sister's brother walked out of that burial chamber. The Holy Spirit transported him out.

Not to be redundant, the Author of Life said, "Loose him and let him move." (John 11: 44). What a charming mystical picture of humanity being born in iniquity and spiritually lifeless, not going anywhere because of sin. (Romans 6: 23, 7: 9). Depravity has confined sinners so they cannot hear non-material things or speak or share the Word of Jehovah-Rophe. The Blessed and Only Ruler loves humankind, but He will not prevent us from the sentence of divine death. (Romans 5: 12).

God has called every believer to the works of righteous service and to give evidence of the Good News of Eternal Life's generosity and mercy; this is true of freedom of speech. Telling the Saints of one's witness plays a crucial role in how they help remove the grave clothes from sinners. Christian interaction is why Paul said: "But nobody's life is more important than them completing their mission. Mission-driven is the ministry we received from the Lord Jesus: to testify regarding the great message of God's compassion." Acts 20: 24.

After sharing the Gospel and individualized testimony, we should ask them to atone for their sins; otherwise, the information is nothing more than empathy. An invocation of repentance shows them how immorality harms them and others around them. The simple prayer below will do the job.

MERCIFUL ALMIGHTY GOD, I COME BEFORE YOU HUMBLED AND MOURNFUL, AWARE OF MY EVIL, AND PREPARED TO ASK FORGIVENESS. LORD, FORGIVE ME, FOR I HAVE SINNED BEFORE YOU. CLEANSE MY TRANSGRESSION, PURIFY ME WITH HOLINESS, AND HELP ME TURN FROM THESE IMMORALITIES. LEAD ME TO WALK IN YOUR PLAN INSTEAD, LEAVING BEHIND MY FORMAL LIFETIME AND STARTING A NEW GENERATION IN YOU. So, I REPENT ALL MY SINS AND GIVE MY LIFE TO YOU. THANK YOU FOR STRIPPING ME OF MY GRAVE CLOTHES AND CLOTHING ME WITH GARMENTS OF RIGHTEOUSNESS.

Repentance is the only alternative to avoid the winding sheet of enslavement. The Messiah's forgiveness replaces wrongdoing with noble deeds, taking believers beyond remorse. God overlooked such ignorance in the past, but now he commands people everywhere to repent (Acts 17: 30).

To keep freedom, we must recognize mistakes and honor the right to worship, as secular and Biblical history shows. "If we claim to be without sin, we deceive ourselves, and the truth is not in our denial. "But if we confess the faults, the Redeemer is faithful and will forgive our misdeeds and purify individually from all unrighteousness," First John 1: 8–9.

Chapter 5

GRAVEN IMAGES HINDERS FREEDOM

The words graven images are a discredited supposition used in the Old and New Testaments to show cult statues and promote non-Christian faith. Pagan empires deprived individuals of freedom, according to the Holy Scriptures. These people repeatedly tied themselves to disobedience and worshiped erroneous gods.

The Bible teaches that anything which replaces Jehovah is a false idol. (Jeremiah 10:10, John 17: 3, 1 Thessalonians 1: 9, and 1 John 5: 20). Also, see Jeremiah 2: 25-35.

God repeatedly forgave and rescued His people as they worshiped pagan symbols. JEHOVAH-JIREH used the HORN of SALVATION to declare freedom and deliver the Israelites from slavery in Egypt. THE FATHER sent His Son to the planet to free humanity from the sin of spiritual slavery leading to death. However, He wanted to convey His point to His supporters about His human God's Nature.

For instance, when Jesus came to the region of Caesarea Philippi, he asked his disciples, "Who do people say the Son of Man is?" They replied, "Some say John the Baptist; others say Elijah; and others,

Jeremiah or (another prophet)." "But what about you?" he asked. " Who do you suppose I am? Simon Peter answered. You are the Christ, the Son of the living God. Jesus responded, "Blessed are you, Simon's offspring of Jonah; Jehovah revealed this to you not man but by my Father in heaven." Matthew 16: 13–17.

Then, in John 8: 36, the Author of Life makes a beautiful statement of victory. He says, "If the Hope of Glory sets you at liberty, you will be free indeed." So here is the question: why would anyone take off the salvation of honor to wrap themselves in the grave clothes of the dead? And cease their power to act, speak, or think as they want without impediment or restraint.

"Garment of Praise" symbolizes joy and blessing from Jehovah-Jireh (Nehemiah 8:10).

But what has the Man from Heaven freed humankind from since their existence? The writer's question is rhetorical. Humanity was in bondage until Christ paid for our sins. It was the grave clothes of lawlessness (humanity confinement).

The Bible tells us that the wicked man's evil deeds ensnare him; the cords of his sin hold him fast. He will die for lack of discipline, led astray by his great folly (Proverbs 5: 22–23 NIV84). The impulses of sinful immorality take captive, bound to the instincts of the wrappings of the dead. Thus, humans had no power to overcome the influence of dishonorably. So, unrighteousness is yet humanity's Ruler and gladly holds them hostage.

Thus, during this age of Christianity, the path to liberation appears as a haughty fable to the followers of the Savior in the world. And the culture of sin has made Christianity insensible. But the Scriptures are still the most efficient weapon to simplify the meaning of emancipation. The Bible shows how redemptive independence collapses radical secular theories.

The Christian Bible gives righteous ideas, effective decisions, and hopeful memories. "For THE WORD of GOD is living and active. Sharper than any double-edged sword, it penetrates even to dividing soul and spirit, joints, and marrow; it judges the intentions and attitudes of the heart" (Hebrews 4: 12 NIV84). Jesus says those who continue in the Father's Commandment He frees from the slavery of sin (John 8: 31). So, authentic democracy is not a commodity one buys but a gift from THE REDEEMER; it is grace that only the Son of David can give.

Self-governance is a way of life provided by Divine inheritance. From accepting the Lamb Without Blemish, every soul is wandering around in the cerecloth of Lazarus; they are the walking dead because of their transgression issues. So, long-suffering is challenging because the unsaved society is still sinning. Yet it requires courage in the obvious ways, like being brave enough to share your faith with them.

The lost souls are eating, drinking, and doing all the righteous are doing. Spiritual realism sees people living without salvation as mummies wrapped in burial garments. The Bible considers the redemptive asleep to depravity but alive to the All-Merciful Hope of Mercy, Romans 6:11.

Jesus said, "I am the way, the truth, and the life. No one comes to the Father except through me." John 14: 6 (NIV84). The First-Born desires the Saints to glorify Him through the Written Word. The Bible is a reminder of righteousness for Christians. For unburdened salvation, Christ has set us free. In Galatians 5:1, Paul urges the Christians to stand firm and not burden themselves with slavery, as he wrote under the Holy Spirit's anointing.

Those who follow the Lord consider themselves part of a greater mission to uphold and spread righteousness worldwide. Iniquity leads to enslavement unless one accepts Jesus Christ as Lord and Savior. Except sinners absorb themselves into their prison of pride. Approaching the Maker of Heaven and Earth brings eternal compassion.

Therefore, we are nothing more than zombies without Christ. OUR FATHER's act of raising Christians to divine life doesn't guarantee that believers will be free from their wretched grave clothes. The All-Wise instituted a Spiritual Law at the universe's inception, stating that sin leads to death because all humans are sinners. But the GOOD NEWS for the Saints is they constantly live in THE LORD'S presence.

Chapter 6

RESURRECTION POWER BRINGS FREEDOM

After the Hope of Glory restoration to life, He assigned His disciples to call the lost transgressors out of the immoral acts of cynicism (Isaiah 55: 11). Saints strive to promote God's righteousness without seeking attention for themselves.

The Messiah says that His BEGETTER is THE SHINING LUMINESCENCE, and no obscurity is in Him, nor should there be any absence of Holy radiance in His followers. The Son of the Almighty revealed His Father's brightness in this mysterious realm.

When Jesus declared, "Let your righteous illumination glow before the world," that was not the complete verse. He explained why: "So that they may know your valuable skills and show the Grandeur of The Father in paradise" (Matthew 5: 16).

Jesus is THE LAMB of the Author of All Things. So, THE LORD was absent of any blemish or gloom. But He, being The First Born of the Dead, is empathetically showing up at the dark catacomb mind of any sinner. "Display your good works so others can praise Jehovah" - He urges His Saints (Matthew 5:16).

The Redeemer desires worshippers to bring new life to sinners' hearts. See Ezekiel 36: 26. Christians must share the value of salvation for a relationship with God and eternal life in heaven. But in your hearts, set apart Christ as Savior. Always be vigilant to answer everyone who asks you to explain your hope. But do it with gentleness and respect (1 Peter 3: 15).

Believers witnessing changes sinners' attitudes to joy and gratitude. Saints help sinners break free from Satan's hold, recover from shame, and turn away from misery. Therefore, salvation by accepting Jesus Christ creates eternal liberation, redemptive rehabilitation, and faultless security. In addition, He allows us to experience His Love and Authority today in the radiance of Sacred Holiness.

"I am not ashamed of the Gospel because of the power of God for the redemption to everyone who believes: first for the Jew, then for the Gentile," Romans 1:16 (NIV84).

However, when the Glorified do not obey the great commission, Matthew 28: 18-20, they contribute to the inaction of the souls who will perish devoid of Christ. These individuals could spend eternity in agony. Yet, fear is the most significant deterrent when followers talk to sinners regarding witnessing the Gospel.

Various believers feared losing relationships by sharing their true feelings about religion. Still, Jesus' instructions to go to the earth and create disciples were not just for His skilled clergy members; they applied to the righteous generations. But that does not mean that sharing one's faith is easy. Although we rely on the Holy Spirit, arming oneself with basic communication skills helps witness.

Regardless, the Exalted must never forget:

> *"Flawless adoration drives out fear because consternation has to do with punishment. The Lord's people's fears are not perfect in the heart's affair" (1 John 4: 18).*

So, even the righteous may worry about evangelizing. Wear the armor of faith and hope (Colossians 1:5). The punishment will be worse without faith.

THE LORD assigned His souls only to show the loss of eternality because the walking dead can do nothing for themselves. Again, God's Supreme Mercy in delivering undeserved reprobates brings Him Glory. Christ's effort is to provide for the lost. Hell-bound transgressors are the root of the Gospel and are the fundamental margin of the Ecclesiastical Word. Sinners need the salvation of Jesus Christ to rescue them from a destiny worse than death.

"God made you alive with His Son when you were dead in your sins and in the uncircumcision of your sinful nature. He forgave every sin" (Colossians 2:13). Now, we must show others the way of everlasting life.

Many Christians prefer to practice their beliefs but worry they cannot answer all questions. They tell themselves they need to study more. The writer has shared his passion for Christ for over 50 years and always admits more to learning. Nobody ever feels 100% ready to take Holiness's marketing steps. We must trust the Holy Ghost in what intimidates us relative to witnessing and do it by faith. Luke 12: 12.

In addition, the Savior said, "Do not be nervous of those who murder the individual but cannot kill the lifeblood. Instead, suspect *THE ONE* who can destroy both souls in hell." (Matthew 10: 28). The King of Kings instructed them to go, what they must do, and speak. "Proclaim this message: the Kingdom of heaven is close. Heal the sick, raise the dead, cleanse those who have leprosy, drive out demons. Freely you have received; liberally give." (Matthew 10: 6-8). Then, He challenged them, "Do not be afraid!"

But the Marthas of the world are crying, "Let the departed be, believing a foul odor beneath the sinner's unresponsive cloth of unrighteousness." Yet, the refreshing fragrance of Divine deliverance resurrects, refreshes, and lasts eternally. So, The King of Glory is the Only Savior.

He desires to liberate people from sin, and the Scriptures show that the sole approach to forgiveness is faith in God (John 14: 6). The Son of the Almighty is the only way to salvation for two of ten thousand reasons. (1) THE FATHER chose him to be the Redeemer. (2) Jesus is the only ONE to have come from heaven and returned there again, John 3: 13.

Paul urges the young pastor to pray. The Great High Priest said, "Whoever hears His Word and believes Him who sent Him has eternal existence, and He will not condemn them; they have crossed over from death to life." John 5: 24.

That stated the foremost reason to witness is our love for the Resurrection of Christ. As we contemplate what the Good Shepherd has done for humanity in forgiving their sins, sharing our faith with others should come naturally. The Saint's hearts ought to fracture for the trespassers because immoral acts break the heart of Jesus. Christians are not a cut above the public.

I urge everybody to be prayerful and intercede and make thanksgiving for everyone—1 Timothy 2: 1. "Are we better than sinners?" No, for we charged that Jews and Greeks are under sin; the Bible tells us, " None is righteous, not even one; there is none who understands," and not anyone pleases THE LORD 100%. Study Romans 3: 9-19.

Countless people interpret the Holy Resurrection of the Absolute Being differently in this culture. Salvation is a theological concept based on Jesus' teachings, not political emancipation. Or they select representatives based on personal civic beliefs. Uncountable interpretations can lead the righteous away from THE LORD's message of restoring sovereignty.

The Infinite Spirit's righteousness differs from individualism and their non-confinement of speech. The Bible tells us Christians are unique, but everything belongs to the Almighty. If an individual is a child of the MOST HIGH, they must never view their life as belonging to them. Every condition, place, and relationship is All-Might's property because He earned them with His sacrificial death on the cross.

"Jesus purchased you at a price. SO, Honor Our Lord with your body." (1 Corinthians 6: 20).

"Keep watch over yourselves; the Holy Spirit's flocks have made you overseers. Be shepherds of the Good Shepherd Church, which He bought with HIS BLOOD" (Acts 20:28).

The secular empires have convinced everybody's independence depends on a person's financial stability. I wonder how Moses might describe liberty as he encountered a flooding Red Sea, with Pharaoh's troops in hot pursuit to take his and Israel's lives. As the Pentateuch Lawmaker stood before a body of water, he could not pass over and hopelessly opposed himself.

But for sure, with the threat of his life and the death of the nation of Israel, silver and gold were not his number one interests. Case in point, growing in righteousness is a sequence of problem-solving opportunities. The challenges that the Saints encounter have the potential to either overwhelm them or boost their confidence. But morality is determined by one's moral character and adherence to faith.

Jesus replied, "Because you have so little conviction. I tell you the truth, if you have faith as small as a mustard seed, you can say to this mountain, 'Move from here to there, and it shall be so. Nothing is impossible for you." Matthew 17: 20.

Did you note in Daniel 3 the braveness of Shadrack, Meshach, and Abednego? In a burning incinerator with Jesus, one's perception of disimprisonment may differ from those of these three men. But nothing regarding their demeanor suggests they were anxious or angry against the city of Babylon, which put them in the fiery furnace.

For instance, Daniel's behavior amongst a cage of hungry lions was not fear but Godly calm. Last, what of Lazarus in a frostbitten, dark, damp cave bound with the dead people's clothes? As we can see, everyone has a different interpretation of what civil liberties are to them. Salvation is absolute, and its freedom extends beyond uncaring people who take preeminence of the need to contribute to themselves.

So, what does authentic deliverance resemble? Our Hope promises virtuous emancipation, not individual infatuation. When the Wisdom of God laid bare Himself as the Messiah, He said He had come to the planet to "proclaim and unburdened liberties." (Luke 4: 18), which means the struggle is over for humanity.

The Apostle Paul wrote to the young pastor, Timothy. He needed encouragement to continue to fight the good campaign of faith. It is every Christian work to release sinners from their grave clothes. So, they may lay hold on to eternal life (1 Timothy 6:12). The Scripture shows that the Godman (Christ) is the root of Christian's liberation and spiritual morality for evangelism (Ephesians 6: 11-12).

Witnessing the GOOD NEWS is the best way to encourage sinners to embrace eternal qualities. The Saints should use the Bible to create opportunities to do good. Heed the Holy One's directions before giving aid. For example, a sizeable crowd accompanied Jesus to the sepulture of Lazarus to console Martha. But the RESTORATION to LIFE came to show the POWER of RESURRECTION.

Jehovah's power brings us into a relationship with the Righteous Branch. Paul wrote, "This authority ordinarily takes place in suffering." (Philippians 3: 10). Paul's speech regarding his time on earth is interchangeable with the Horn of Salvation's Existence (Philippians 3:

11). He explains Jesus' standard of living by drawing a parallel between his continuous struggle and the challenges faced by the LORD of ALL.

Our comprehension of the Divine can assist us in conquering life's obstacles and fortifying our bond with the Supreme Being. So, the Messiah Restoration Power proves:

- The Gospel is true
- Immanuel is the Son of God
- The Author of Salvation pours the Hallowed Spirit out into the souls of Christians
- It gives the Glorified a living hope

Yes, The Redeemer's death and resurrection are historical; it happened. But doubters are comfortable with their skepticism; they do not realize the supernatural influence Emmanuel instilled within His disciples after the Messiah rose from the grave. So, in worship, the Saints give their attention to Jehovah in a two-way conversation: (1) we talk to Him, (2) listen to Him. When a believer prays in the Name of the Good Shepherd, the authority of the Holy Spirit empowers them to do miraculous works for the kingdom.

On another occasion, the Prince of Peace said, "If the Son sets us at liberty, we are free from restrictions to have the right of self-determination" (John 8: 36). But the doubtful Martha of the world yet sees physical death as resolving to believe. She thought, "Dead Saints will rise when everyone rises on the last day." The busy lady was wrong! But the revelation is this: The end of a time for everybody else is the beginning of eternity with the Living Stone, John 3: 16.

"If anyone is in the Savior, they are righteous creatures: old ideas pass away; behold, objectives become unique" (II Corinthians 5: 17). That means every disciple who puts their faith in the Holy of Holiness is an unusual new creation. They have a forward-thinking attitude towards their lives and careers. So, everything for the moralistic is unconventional!

Our most important responsibility as Christians is to live for Jesus Christ. The Bible clarifies Jesus came to this earth to save the lost. Being born of God is one of the essential characteristics of the new nature of Christ Jesus in a person who has experienced the new birth. A person with the pristine nature of Jesus Christ is a partaker of God's divine nature, making that person concerned about spiritual concepts. However, like most Christians, Martha loved the GODMAN; she spent droves of time with the Alpha and Omega. He ate at her table and slept in her house. But she understood not Him as the RESURRECTOR WHO breathes new life into the dead.

Do the Saints, like Martha, focus too much on serving and forget to worship the Prince of Peace? Usually, when the Glorified genuinely senses their need for the resurrected Lord, they are available for Him. Otherwise, Christians get so busy they do not read their Word, pray, or think about the future. Jesus is the only Mediator and only Savior. It is through Him alone that anyone receives the blessings of salvation.

Still, Christlike Followers work and make a living, taking care of the family and their needs. The Saints prioritize these things as the center of their lives. The Resurrector noticed Martha's hectic schedule; hence, He will soon speak to this generation about our need to be available for His teachings. Luke 10: 38-42. Failure to care appropriately for the Christian faith inevitably leads to an empty epitome of Holy compassion.

Worship is the feeling or expression of high esteem and adoration for Jesus's sacrifice for humanity. Acknowledge Jesus Christ's generous potential for expansion and propagation. Believing that the Son of God is enough involves resting in His assurances. As the Children of the Author of All Things settle in His promises, they understand God. Proper rest in Our Lord causes us to centralize ourselves in righteous freedom.

The Divine privilege gives liberty to the heart of the individual. It allows the souls of the devotees to reach unparalleled heights. Not any flesh can rule over them inwardly unless they permit it. When Christians understand virtuous sovereignty, their relationship with the Father grows stronger. Many accept that spiritual entitlement to absolute independence comes from moral character. Righteousness allows us to choose God's self-determination for our lives.

So, true liberation comes alive in Holiness. And should motivate one's most profound persona to righteousness, which cannot be in chains, restrained, or put into a cage. Freedom is only through the resurrected power of Jesus the Redeemer.

For example, Jesus, the Messiah, called in a loud voice, Lazarus, come out! Mummified, the dead man came out of his burial tomb, hands and feet wrapped with strips of linen and a cloth around his face. Then, THE LORD said to them, Take off the tomb outfits and let him go. Removing the burial garments means helping sinners remove their sinful fabric and unrighteous blindfold. Unrighteousness limits knowledge and sight, stopping them from seeking help.

Righteousness enables us to see spiritually and trust in the Lord, not false gods. Grave clothes of the world are hindrances to spiritual power. So, avoid negative concepts such as anger, wrath, malice, blasphemy, and filthy communication. (Colossians 3: 8).

Chapter 7

CHOOSING GRAVE CLOTHES OVER FREEDOM

Not only inexperienced Christians, but we also all have a problem with the garments of ungodliness because of the disobedience of Adam. The Apostle Paul encourages the teen preacher (Timotheus) in 2 Timothy 2: 22. He must "Flee youthful lusts." His instruction to the young pastor implies a wealth of immoralities that primarily constrains the adolescent. For instance, lust is the mummification cloth of iniquity, explicitly exploiting the youth.

Adam transgressed God's Command and precipitated lots of souls to be sinners. Jesus followed God's will, leading to billions of people finding acceptance of God. Redemption is only possible through the sacrifice of Jesus, the Judge of the Living and Dead. He makes virtuous deliverance a completion of the transformational process.

However, the first step in managing the unclean garment of depravity is admitting to having it on the body. We need the Savior, Emanuel, to rescue and redeem us from the confinement of the burial clothing. So, whenever God's followers put on the robe of unrighteousness, it causes them to stumble over sinful obstructions. Intercessory prayer helps keep Saints within Holy bounds.

The Supreme Being helps humans with disputes and improving health, prosperity, and relationships. Specifically, righteous devotion also has its purpose in thanksgiving and praise. Although an individual does not believe in the authority of consecrated invocation, there can be no benefit from Jesus' Divine Goodness. So, talking to THE UNIVERSE'S SOVEREIGN enhances one's distinctive way of life if one trusts Him.

And a person's solemn request expressed to The Creator on somebody else's welfare shall encourage the Saint to move forward. Prayer cannot replace action when someone unhelpful says, "I will pray for your troubles." They mean, "I'll hide in my secret closet, using my plea to the Almighty as an excuse for not aiding with the issue." By all measures, pray, and if the Prince of Peace has given you the means to support them, do so.

Further, no Saint knows when they may fall to the slender end of righteousness. The Bible tells the readers that "all have sinned and come short of the glory of The Deity," but "the gift of Jehovah is eternal life in OUR LORD." (Romans 6: 23). So, every evangelistic soul should lend a hand to carry the overloads for others. Our Christian commitment to each other is to aid one another in believing, overcoming, and remaining resolute in a terrifying world.

For example, great sadness overcomes Jesus while standing at Lazarus' tomb. Overpowered by physical despair, He weeps. Then, he makes what Martha thought was an unreasonable request: "Remove the stone from his burial place." Martha interrupts THE SAVIOR to emphasize that His suggestion was not rational.

Jesus also knew He would die and sleep in a burial space. So, while standing there, He also understood facing death would be a challenge. However, with Jehovah, it is not about humankind's logic. The Christian life is one of obedience.

Every follower of Christ must help to spread the Gospel, regardless of who they are—a pastor, Church member, or student. The Author of the Scriptures is not asking us to save sinners; that is the redeemer's work. However, the human heart is still naturally unclean (Titus 3: 5). Those who share the Gospel represent a pure love that washes away their dirty clothes. They allow God to give them new garments of righteousness.

"See, I have taken your iniquity away from you and will clothe you with festal robes" (Zechariah 3: 4).

The Apostle Paul encouraged Timothy to discard his former way of life. He counseled him to turn away from deceitful desires and renew himself in the Spirit. He wanted him to display a new self-fashioned after the likeness of The Author of All Things, as stated in Ephesians 4: 22-24, because of evil acts.

Still, it seems hopeless sometimes to keep ourselves free from wrongdoings. The temptations' mandates are often too strong for a Saint to overcome alone. But "with God, nothing shall be impossible." (Luke 1: 37). Jesus provides the way to victory over sin. In Him, we have redemption through His blood, the forgiveness of sins, and following the riches of God's grace (Ephesians 1: 7).

In addition, the Bible tells us that no temptation has seized the Saints except what they can stand. The Supreme Being is faithful; he will not allow attacks of what they can bear. But when the desire comes, God would also provide a way out so you may stand up under it (1 Corinthians 10: 13). The only drawback to this Scripture is this: we cannot assist individuals who want no help. Removing grave clothes from folks comfortable in them is a waste of time.

Therefore, we must set reaction limitations with known reprobates. Establishing limits does not mean you should stop loving or praying for them. It is vital to establish boundaries to make them understand your discomfort with their sinful choices. The Holy Spirit will show you when the time is right to help the person not ready for enlightenment about Christ. Keeping ourselves prayerfully for sinners in mind is essential for helping them.

Christians can worship with the help of The Divine Paraclete (1 Corinthians 12:11), who assists them in making their prayers effective. Hence, we speak on the Redeemer's behalf, not on our own. Now that THE SANCTIFIER is living inside believers, they know Him as He conveys gentle notions that are not theirs.

They discover a soft expression deep within them, saying, "This is the way; walk in it," Isaiah 30: 21. Therefore, the Saints need to ponder God's Writs coupled with His Humble Power before witnessing. Then, they should ask THE LORD to disclose to them His Mind. The Glorified individuals comprehend Jehovah's qualities and associate His salvation strategy with righteousness.

We sometimes let our selfishness take over instead of listening to His Ideas. The Maker of All Things Voice always follows what He wrote in the Bible. Jesus spoke, "Blessed are those who listen to THE AUTHORITATIVE BOOK and maintain it." (Luke 11: 28).

The righteous adhere to the Sacred Writings of the Old or New Testaments. So, learning is not the result THE LORD is seeking. The Supreme Being asks His followers to continue in it after receiving it. Romans 10: 17 says that we grow in faith by understanding THE SCRIPTURES of Christ. But whoso keeps HIS WORD, in Him verily is the FATHER'S love perfected: now know that we are in HIM, 1 John 2: 5.

Like all other humans, most relevant souls live with a sinful nature that wants to do their desires, contrary to God's works. So, when the Saints follow the inclinations of the flesh, it causes them to sin. Then, acts of wickedness systematically draw another's thoughts in a hostile direction, not pleasing to the Alpha and Omega.

The apostolic can find solace in the loving-kindness, tender mercies, and patient endurance of their Redeemer, as revealed in His Word. The Prince of Peace leads to joy, contentment, and harmony. So, in witnessing, disciples should not be self-righteous hypocrites.

However, Holiness obligates us to be firm yet speak out of compassion and empathy when calling sinners to repent. As the Great High Priest stated, "The repentance of a single sinner causes great rejoicing in heaven." Even today, consolidating a humble life and a zealous approach persuades a winning spirit for the loss.

In a highly polarizing phase in our country now, the upright must conduct themselves in a manner worthy of the Gospel of The Good Shepherd. So, each time the followers of Christ metaphorically give in to the flesh, we discover ourselves back in the tomb of Lazarus, wrapped in a burial shroud. The sinful catacomb is dark, and the grave clothes of unrighteousness are uncomfortable.

The Glorified have become so accustomed to the powerful scent of immortality. They needlessly criticize others, have unproductive fantasies of sexual misconduct, and consider greed. And feel disheartened about their virtuous existence. Next, they wonder where the Savior is in this and if He cares about them.

But in God's Word, we read about how His love for humanity is immense and how His hatred for evil is colossal. So, because of the consequences of wickedness, God sent His only Son to earth. As a human, His mission was to separate His people from the cloth of the deceased.

It is why the Holy Spirit forever raised Jesus from a lifeless Body as proof of His enormous victory to free humankind from the agony of eternal extinction. Still, repentance is necessary for salvation. After deliverance, the saved must continue to repent or change their minds about contemplating or committing sin. Remember, none of us is perfect.

Paul advised the believers to act wisely with outsiders and avoid unrighteousness. "Let our speech always be with grace, as though seasoned with salt, so that you will know how to respond to each person" (Colossians 4: 5-6).

The belief in the Heir of All Things empowers individuals to choose a righteous living instead of being confined to eternal cessation. The Bible assures its readers that those who refrain from evil will conquer sin and death in their lives. Hence, Immanuel proudly acknowledges them as His siblings- Hebrews 2: 11.

Eventually, Jesus will return, appearing in the clouds to raise all His followers to spend eternity with Him in heaven. That is Jehovah's plan for the Saints, but impure ideas, discouragement, anger, criticism, and vanity still fascinate us. Our sinful nature controls it and can never please THE LORD. It is why believers often feel they cannot avoid the tomb of Lazarus or his grave clothes. We are born with a sinful nature inherited from Adam and Eve, which leads us to defy Jehovah. (Psalms 51: 5).

God is faithful and provides a way out of temptation, as seen in 1 Corinthians 10:13. The way out of immoral acts is how the Horn of Salvation taught His followers. When the shroud of the departed traps us, we must fervently implore the Almighty who saved the Firstborn of the Dead with His Divine Reverence (Hebrew 5: 7).

During worship, the Humble Comforter exposes the hidden sin in one's flesh and then shows how to be independent (1 Peter 4: 1-3). So, how desperate are we to be separated from the lifeless wrappings of mummified sinners? Have you prayed for the filling of the Divine Spirit to have the strength to deny and overcome the cave of Lazarus?

The disciples said to Jesus, "Teach us to pray." The Scripture teaches it is uncomplicated for the Author of All Things to answer our request. We invite the God of the Universe into our situation during the Saint's extraordinarily powerful divine sanction. Prayer converts people and changes conditions, but sacred consecration revolutionizes the intercessor. Through worship service with The Master, believers can reach their overall relationship with The Great High Priest.

A note: the disciple's request to teach them to pray was: "Lord, show us how to stay out of the dead cave." As Christians mature in sanctification, they understand they come alive and more engaged with what the First Cause is doing. We cannot be perfect, but our moral influence grows as we strive for righteousness. The All-Powerful will move mountains and transform worshippers into people of love, joy, and peace. So, during times of temptation, the Glorified must seek Divine Sanction.

Therefore, the key to individual Christian freedom is to set themselves and the dead (unsaved) free before reaching their tomb. The Bible tells us that when Jesus came to Lazarus' grave, He looked up to the Father; I thank You; You have heard Me. The Alpha and Omega were not praying a redundant prayer, but He told this to benefit the people standing there so they may believe Jehovah sent Him. The Bible guarantees that prayer can help us find real peace of mind. Study Philippians chapter 4: 6, 7.

Chapter 8

FREEDOM IN CHRISTIAN UNITY

Each Parishioner's Talent Is Valuable and Essential for The Local Church.

In studying Nehemiah's third division, we realized the metropolis of Jerusalem favored twelve gates. The gateways controlled the movement of individuals, keeping the municipal center independent. Though, miscellaneous entryways by title were more distinguished by name than others. Given the vocational construction work, the writer would have chosen the Fountain Gate rather than the Dung Gateway as a work project.

However, from a building and tactical viewpoint, no thresholds to the capital were fragile or unessential. All twelve entranceways were significant in strength and functional purpose. Although the faith community is worldwide, with billions of members, we are still social creatures. We can accomplish great and magnificent works when we put our efforts together in righteous harmony.

For instance, in Genesis, chapter eleven is the Biblical account of the Tower of Babel; the individuals had bound their strength to raise a metropolis and superstructure to Heaven. And THE LORD came down to see the place and the building. According to Jehovah, the people are obstacle-free and in perfect harmony to achieve their goals. We will confuse their vocabulary, so they may not understand each other's conversation. And all humanity was of a single dialect. So, He scattered them abroad on the face of the world, and they stopped construction on their high rise.

Humankind disrespected the Supreme Being by taking it upon themselves to establish a structure to avoid a second flood. But the King of Kings said He would not destroy the earth by water again but by fire. They blasphemed Jehovah, so He divided the individuals into linguistic groups. He confused the workers by introducing different dialects. As we can see in these Scriptures, societies may accomplish much when they unite.

The Glorified God-given mission is to "carry each other's burdens." Solidarity among the Ecclesiastics strengthens the community. A unified House of Jehovah offers the power of the Gospel. Sadly, The Lord's people who ignore unity limit growth. Each believer has the natural ingenuity to feel at home as they exercise their state of harmony in purpose. Yet, our work can often be useless and inflexible, but the time and talent we give to unify the believers play massive fringe benefits in kingdom building.

A disciple will not reach their potential as leaders until they learn to follow someone else's dream. It is incumbent upon the staff and laypersons to accept the Senior Pastor's observations or departure.

It is a bold statement, but the only way the congregation can grow in righteousness is by pastoral leadership. God has anointed the Local Pastor as the assembly leader. When personalities are at war with the lead shepherd, missions fall by the wayside. Holy perception builds humility and numerical and spiritual growth by submitting to serve others.

Evangelicals must go beyond the four walls of the sanctuary. For instance, THE WALL in Nehemiah Chapter 3 coordinates to form one powerful unit only after the individuals unify under a single goal. "It is good and pleasant when the brothers work simultaneously in agreement," Psalm 133: 1.

Redemption encourages building honest relationships between Christians and non-Christians. And plant Churches in every country and teach the people to obey all that The Messiah commanded (Matthew 28: 18-20). Jesus said, "Launch out into the deep" Luke 5: 4.

Ephesians 4 tells the readers, "There is a single body in partnership with the Spirit, just as God called His followers cohesively to hope in Him only." So, when Christians learn to worship undivided, the world will follow. A larger perspective of redemption causes putting aside strife.

Unity motivates the Church to face all the false reasons believers used to look down on people void of salvation. But disunity triggers the Saints to live in a religious bubble of misconceptions, an illusion of believing they are better than sinners.

A Saint's isolation from the world's sin problems makes us classify our sins as trivial. Christians must open their hearts to the accord of equality that the Biblical writers envisioned, "we are our brother's keepers" Genesis 4: 1-13. As the Saints unite under righteousness, they face a mysterious truth about themselves; we have more in common with the people we disagree with because unanimity allows everybody to experience the beauty of freedom.

Christianity relies on teamwork. Everyone's contribution is necessary to cultivate a bountiful outcome. So, we ought to encourage each other to build and support an evangelistic culture where parishioners trust and respect each other. Then, the Local Church can achieve the foremost and fastest by helping others succeed. When God's people stand united, the sin problem will resolve itself.

After this, THE LORD appointed couples and dispatched them by twos to every town and place where he was about to go, Luke 10: 1.

The Gospel writer gives evidence that Our Great Redeemer framed the ministry of His disciples as teamwork achievers. The Savior called the twelve to him, sent them out two by two, and gave them authority over evil spirits Mark 6: 6-7. Training believers in small groups is skillful. The team tutoring approach shows that the righteous can encourage and empower those they study, serve, and travel together. Jesus used encouragement and discipline to educate his supporters.

For example, humans are born from birth to connect with others. Believers feel connected to their Protestant siblings when they learn Spiritual Values together. The Local Church must embrace unity and righteousness to succeed in holistic Christianity. Elders must teach Evangelism and Christ-focused Dogma to promote responsible faith.

However, the opening Scripture above shows that Jesus' representatives there are power in unity. Paul urged the Glorified to live transparently and achieve sanctification together. A Holy nation should move beyond worship and overcome selfishness with Agape Love. The faithful are duty-bound to covenant righteousness with other Christians: study Hebrews 4: 1-16.

Let us inspire one another to be devoted to good works. Don't neglect to meet, but encourage each other, especially as the Day of Judgment approaches. The witness of a single disciple could only accomplish so much. Christ-centeredness can create a righteous movement for spiritual freedom. The faithful will only reach their common alliance goals if they effectuate an atmosphere to address disunity.

Teamwork collapses barriers blocking Christianity. A believer's Holy imagination has a special meaning or a useful purpose. Yet, unbelievers are skeptical of the claims void of external objects or spiritual concepts unobserved to the senses. For instance, when humankind only naturally trusts what they can see, they cannot evaluate self-confidence.

Faithlessness destroys any chance of a close relationship with Jehovah. Likewise, a believer who walks by sight rather than conviction is a deadly code of belief because it does not lead to a redemptive course of action. Trusting the Supreme Being leads to togetherness, blessings, and rewards for Sainthood. It is an expedition that will allow collaboration among the Immortal as they experience the Most High's fullness of grace and mercy. Righteous union with THE LORD is exhilarating and life-altering.

The House of Worship helps Jehovah's followers to stay united and maintain their ecumenism. The Bible is straightforward: *"Five of you will chase a hundred, and a hundred of you will chase ten thousand, and your enemies will fall by the sword before you." Leviticus 26: 8 (NIV84).* Five is more significant than one. Unanimity allows for a collective agreement on what is morally acceptable.

Satan fears an assembly of righteousness. So, the devil's number one approach is to bring disunity to the world's most robust institution (The Bride of Christ). Trusting in the Savior's Words, "I will build my Church on this rock," is necessary for the Saints.

In Matthew 18:19, the Infinite Spirit emphasized the significance of unity. The Creator meant what He said: "If we agree about anything in prayer, The Author of All Things provides it." So, the Saints must stop limiting THE LORD'S Holy Writ.

Again, the Word also says one would drive off a thousand. Two shall run off ten thousand because the King of kings has sold our enemies to His Glorified (Deuteronomy 32: 20). This Scripture reminds us to work together for righteousness and praise THE LORD for His grace and mercy.

God's Spirit sanctifies disciples, helping them to solve daily problems. But since unification is power, the devil does his best to publicize separation among denominations. But spiritual awakening has always started with Christian solidarity. "This is what the Lord says: Look, an army is coming from the land of the north; a great nation is being stirred up from the ends of the earth:" see Jeremiah 6: 22.

Hence, the Bride of the Loving Father cries for this generation. "My wailings are constant for you!" The faith community of the Righteous Branch. My tears are falling much for you! So, when should our fight be not with each other but for one another? How can we ever unify and build a future worthy of these generations?

Must we stop blame-shifting and point sinners to the Good Shepherd? If we cannot collaborate in sanctification, The Ruler of Heaven and Earth said: "A house divided against itself, that building cannot stand," Mark 3: 25. And every kingdom split eventually comes to desolation, Matthew 12: 25.

The Church's real enemy is no other Christians but Satan, who stands on the mountaintop of sin and claims victory. "I appeal to you, brothers, to watch out for those who cause divisions and create obstacles contrary to the doctrine; avoid them. For such persons do not serve our Lord Christ, but their appetites, and by smooth talk and flattery they deceive the hearts of the naïve," Romans 16: 17-18.

Synergism is more intuitive than disunity. Saints that love and unite appreciate those who share their space. Finding qualified leaders is a struggle for Local Churches.

Selecting the wrong people, from sweeping the floor to teaching a class or overseeing the finances, could be a disaster. The faith community cannot afford to choose unsuitable persons to run God's business. If we feel like an auxiliary leader was a terrible mistake, immediately remedy this unfortunate situation. Note there are ten reasons you want to replace this person:

1. They cannot do the job
2. Damages membership relationships
3. Destroys congregation morale
4. Always make mistakes
5. They only do the minimum
6. Is negative
7. Complains about everything
8. Projects an unprofessional appearance around a Christian persona
9. They are not collaborators
10. They cause disunity among other parishioners

Although we value all our esteemed members, lacking essential skills can lead to expensive errors. Their incompetence will frequently add to the frustration of Pastors and fellowship leaders. When there is pressure to fill a spot quickly, it often results in choosing the wrong individual—where the trouble begins. Keeping that person in that situation can cause severe consequences for the congregation. Unqualified staff can negatively affect morale and the Church's belief in sanctification.

So, once again, when we recognize the problem, we confront the issue right away. The leadership's job is to investigate the best way to pilot it and then run damage control. Often, Christian leaders have the impatience of Abraham. The All-Powerful promised him a son, but he interacted with Hagar instead of waiting. His decision brought disunity to the world even today. Listen, if God called you to a pastorship, He would provide the people gifted to make that administrative department blossom. Yet, we must have tolerance and wait on THE LORD.

Even a little snippet of wrong appointments causes a ripple in the congregation. However, removing anyone from a spiritual leadership position may hurt. So, please do not add to the mistake by mistreating or ignoring the parishioner's feelings. Being insensitive establishes the supervision to look more like jerks. Insensitivity is upsetting and a brush-off that feels the same as an attack. It is enough to make parishioners never want to put themselves out there again.

Christianity makes a boatload of stops, collecting hundreds of thousands of people. As uncountable of these folks unite with the body of Christ, they try to implant their erroneous heresy when they see cracks in Christian education (Acts 8: 9-24). Peter and John stood firm in their faith and adherence to Christ's teachings while managing Simon, the sorcerer. Today's Christians must also stand for righteousness, or the impure followers will create a schism in the Divine.

Afterward, disputes in the congregation become a common source of disagreement in the household of prayer. Then, sinful discord spins off problems such as gossip, pride, and fear, compromising The Word of God to cater to the world. When the orthodox fiddles with matters leading to division, the sum is conflict.

The Saints will stay on track with their ideology of dissidence when grounded in Holiness and Christian teachings. Nobody can say, "Jesus is Lord," except by the Holy Spirit.

The Apostle Paul shows in his two Scriptures the wisdom of unbiased truth. They further acknowledge that the Light of the World is the eternal second member of the Trinity; hence, He is The All-Powerful incarnate. He gave HIS LIFE a substitute for humankind's atonement.

Christian contentment comes from THE REDEEMER, even in the face of false teachers. After defeating all evil, the Holy Spirit brought the Lord of Our Righteousness back to life. According to Ephesians 1:20-22, the Almighty now reigns over all reality independently. Remarkably, the Saint's faith rests in resurrection convictions of the Prince of Peace's teachings.

Speaking with one voice does not mean expressing or communicating only a single opinion. Parishioners could have various aspects of every problem. The dissimilarity of views in the Church of the Messiah is always rewarding. But absent the sacrificial death of the Lamb of God on the cross. Hence, various perspectives and responses may pose a challenge if they contradict "Salvation in Jesus Christ only," as stated in Acts 4:12.

Jesus is the Way, truth, and Life.

So, people who object to the Saviors' Gospel of being the only way of redemption say Christianity is arrogant and full of pride. But they cannot deny the theological basis of Christian principles. The principles are not bound to any situation or culture, and their applicability is timeless. Specifically, the Scripture applies to both Christian and secular audiences.

Unity and forgiveness are the goals of salvation for Christians' freedom. Jehovah, THE LORD, assumed humanity's sin as a replacement. So, His sacrificial death requires humankind to repent. They must have faith in the Scriptures and mutual understanding to validate this independence.

There is not one hope for righteous restoration. Inconsistency in Christian teachings can damage credibility. Still, reading the Hallowed Book can be challenging to understand. But Christianity offers educational tools for Biblical interpretation. Study Bibles provide insight and application for the Scriptures.

Several tools are available to make Bible study more straightforward to understand. The author has adopted RSV, Concordance, Scripture Apps, Holy Writ Software, and Commentaries. Though be careful with extensive compositions, they can be misleading. The author recommends running them by the Churches' education department before buying. However, the writer uses The Thompson Chain Reference Bible for much of his research. And for those who want to probe more profoundly, THE WORD OF GOD, Doctor Bingham Sr., suggests the study of hermeneutic principles and pedagogy concepts.

Engaging with the fellowship is to evade incongruous opinions from multiple Christian figures. The solution to minimizing disinformation is to have a single voice on God's birth, death, and resurrection, the Son. Different Christian teachings can impede Church unity. And how The Perfected Humanity's ultimate self-deprivation benefits humankind these days.

The Apostle Paul wrote: "To walk worthy of our calling in the Good Shepherd. So, members of the Church's body should move diligently to keep the inner nature free, which holds believers together." Ephesians 4: 1-3. Christian unity is a crucial doctrinal interest that demands diligent effort. We must address inadequate agreement in the place of worship with Scriptural research.

So, why is constructive collaboration critical for righteous persuasion? Because the King of Kings is the Incarnate Word WHO unifies Trinitarian Divinity, there is "The Single Essential Being, The Lord, and Father of all," Ephesians 4: 4-6. Jesus passionately prayed that His followers would be one, too (John 17:21, 23). By loving others, as Jesus loved us, we show our discipleship to Him.

Not to be redundant, but harmony within the faith community testifies to the unanimity of the Messiah Triune Oneness. "For three that testify: The Spirit, the water and the blood; and the Triad agree," 1 John 5: 7–8. Note that the Trio has a consensus on purpose, which should be equal in the house of prayer. Regardless, when the Saints conduct their business in disunity, it shows an inaccurate picture of the unsaved.

So, unity in spreading the Word is "an individual hope, Faith in Our Redemption, and One sanctification in Him" Ephesians 4: 4-6. The three must testify to the Holy Writ. The Church of the Living God cannot have different beliefs that save. There is no secular baptism, which symbolizes the Galilean's death, burial, and resurrection.

Congregants should put aside their pride and emotion to follow the Church's mission. Parishioners communicating and understanding one another project a perfect vision of God. Everyone may act, speak, and change without limitation.

The Apostle Paul was prosecuting the case against the Judaizer's false theory in the above Scripture. They claimed: "Galatia Christians must keep the Old Testament before fully knowing true vindication in the God the Son" (Galatians 2: 4).

The evangelist reiterated his assertion that atonement is available for Gentiles. He used Scripture and logic to show how The Nazarene brings complete restoration.

Listen, the Holy Spirit baptizes every believer in the Absolute Being so that they may live righteously in Him. We should confidently approach God's throne to receive mercy and find grace to help us in our time of need.

Temptation can overpower even the most devoted, causing them to forget God's love (Romans chapter Eight reminds us). Accepting God's grace during tough times requires only willingness, not extraordinary perfection. "Ask, and HE yearns to give; seek, and you can find, knock, and THE LORD will open it." Matthew 7: 7.

Apart from obeying the prophets' predictions, what is its significance when forgiveness is a better option, according to Romans 7:7? Still, God's righteous requirement in the Old Creed should stand firm and honored. It proves how sinful humanity is. But as His chosen sinned increasingly, Jehovah's extraordinary grace became more abundant" (Romans 5: 20).

The Apostle assured the Gentiles they could unify with other believers in the Almighty through the Good Shepherd. The Redeemer shows no merit distinction between His people. Instead, The Bible teaches us that the Ruler of Heaven and Earth created all humankind nondiscriminatory. Note that there are four essential facts we ought to understand about individual consensus:

1. Genesis 1: 26-Every human, the Divine Providence, made in His image
2. John 3: 16 THE LORD loves Everybody
3. Romans 3: 23 All humans are sinners
4. Revelation 22: 17every sinner is redeemable

Christianity is not dependent on political views. The state of the Saints' amalgamation directly results from the Gospel. Therefore, the Spiritual union does not describe the prestigious positions in the Local Church.

THE LORD could call any Glorified soul to fill a life of good works. That being so, unanimity is an account of a believer's impartial merit in the eyes of the Author of all things and how we respect His Holy Nature and each other. In addition, the entire Christian nation is in Christ; thus, we are all one.

Slavery, racism, xenophobia, and partiality have always been a problem for humankind, as it was during Jesus' day. Hatred rhetoric divides Christians when it's present in the Local Church. Therefore, hate is an unrestrained physical and mental exertion that triggers extreme emotions.

The author defines Christocentric disunity as resentment. For instance, the Jewish nation has no higher rank than the Greeks or non-Jews. Christianity views no ethnicity as superior to an enslaved person. And righteousness does not view men as superior to women. Galatians 3: 28.

Still, the upright can often look at what they have achieved in a broken world and think of themselves as better than someone with less. Could the love of their possessions be more significant than that of God's faithful? As an example, the writer succeeded as a seminary leader by assembling a team of parishioners who were more intelligent than he was. For unification and freedom, the Saints must not allow their ego to impede choosing the best individuals for the mission. Always remember, in Christ, there are no superior humans or any inferior.

Salvation brings fairness, independence, and freedom to all individuals. So, how is this possible when the world is in such disarray? All followers of the Triad Union unite under The Most-High. Note that none can be more noteworthy or inconsequential. All the Saints are with moral distinction in the eyes of God.

Divine unity is all about how Christian's care for someone else. But disunity at any level of the morally acceptable is unfriendly. The righteous should teach novice believers to resist human desires and put others first. For the fundamental unselfish, they must serve in God's world regardless of what they have, where a person is from, their skin color, or who they betrothed. A new command I give you is to be complete with each other. As I have loved you, so cherish each other. All men will know you are my disciples if you relish one another (John 13: 34–35).

Jesus' teachings showed the importance of faithfulness in Christian unification. The Saints show charitable compassion, unlike the world's sinful people. Note that the amalgamation of affection influences The Local and the universal Church. Further, intimidation is not an issue for strong, influential leaders by intelligent people; they embrace their intellect.

Chapter 9

FREEDOM IN CHRISTIAN ELECTION

THE LORD'S righteous act of deliverance is absolute because He does not rely on outside help besides His OWN consecrated wisdom. Predestination is God's decision to choose those who accept Jesus's redemption. Human laws do not affect God's choice of predestination.

In preference to homo sapiens restoration, every living soul in life comes into the world under the banner of spiritual death. (Ephesians 2: 1-3). The sinner cannot respond to righteousness in their fallen state and, therefore, cannot choose the Holy of Holies, obey Him, or even please Him. The earthborn mind of the unbelievers "is hostile toward the Savior, for it does not subject itself to the Law of Author of All Things. (Romans 8: 7-8).

So, this is what the Messiah meant in John 6: 44, when He said, "No person can come to Me unless the Father who sent Me draws him." The Prince of Peace adopted Christians and predestined them as sons of righteous passion. Through the Almighty SON, Christ, as an inheritance to do good works after the counsel of His will." We read In Acts 13:

48, "When the Gentiles heard THE WORD, they rejoiced and glorified God because the Supreme Being CHOSE them to eternal life."

Acts 16:14 tells us, "Jehovah saved Lydia after hearing Scriptures, THE INFINITE SPIRIT opened her heart to RESPOND to the things written by the Everlasting."

Paul used the Old Testament to illustrate Christian selection: Rebekah's children were from the same ancestor, Isaac. God chose the younger twin before they were even born. As Jehovah said: "Jacob I loved, but Esau I hated," Romans 9: 10–13. So why did THE MASTER detest the older brother? The quick answer is that we do not know, but we can theorize by applying hermeneutical principles to the text.

Note that the writer understood hatred from the K J V Sacred Writ. It has two meanings: (1) a feeling of intense disapproval for somebody as a verb. (2) It is an extreme antagonism to get even as a noun. But the New King James Version and The American Standard translation translate enmity as " to cherish less." See Genesis 29: 31-33.

Genesis 37:3 highlights THE LORD's favoritism for specific individuals, like Jacob's father-in-law's youngest daughter. Selecting one child does not mean resentment towards the other.

Jacob cared for both Laban's daughters, but his love for the younger girl was essential to his own. Decisively, unrestricted passion is the highest form of Godly grace. Isaac had untethered compassion for Leah, but Rachel had a place of a lesser amount of importance. So, the word hate signifies limited in Greek and Hebrew languages. Yet, the intensity of infatuation is still deep and emotional, but obscure. Saints God chooses for Agape missions, and He connects their souls to Him, which goes beyond themselves.

Look closer at Malachi chapter 1: 1-3. (Paraphrase) I treasured Jacob, but am not enthusiastic about Esau, his brother. Also, "I have cherished you," THE LORD answers. "But you ask, 'How have you cared for us?' to undervalue the King of Kings' mercies and justify the hateful offenses they asked. "Was not Esau Jacob's blood twin, yet You favored one over another?"

Again, the Deity valued both siblings, but He gave the younger son a unique inheritance that carries eternal salvation. The Gospel confirms this in Luke 14: 26 and gives the readers a better understanding of the Hebrew Scriptures. "If anyone comes to me but loves his father, mother, wife, children, brothers, or sisters—or even life—more than me, he cannot be my disciple. Whoever is unwilling to carry his cross and follow me cannot be my follower."

Jesus was not teaching His Glorified to dislike or despise our family; He wanted us to embrace each other with sacrificial compassion, "A new commandment I give to you, that you care for every believer" (John 13: 34).

So, the excerpt, "Esau I have hated," irritates many Saints. But the righteous should understand this idiom not as a statement of feeling or attitude, but as a legal term. Tradition has it a father who used the hate terminology as a legitimate concept to distribute his properties was his choice. The rebuffed offspring received resources to make their way. But the preferred heir inherited everything.

In Romans 9: 6-7, 9: 10–13, Paul the crusader is unwavering in opposing doubts about the unfavorable reference from the Savior Who had failed in His Election promises to Israel. He emphasizes his statement by contrasting Jews and Gentiles who understand God's all-powerful authority.

The Judaistic race does not promise redemption or a birthright. Only THE FATHER may designate everlasting sanctification.

Paul contrasts Jewish tradition with grace in Genesis 25: 21–26. He illustrates the birth of Isaac's two sons. God does not guarantee natural descendants favoring the firstborn. Because he chose the younger son to be the descendant of righteousness. (See Genesis 15: 4–6).

Various theologians misunderstand Paul's teachings on predestination. They split hairs; the Supreme Being accepts innumerable people for never-ending salvation and others for perpetual damnation. Not so! The Holy Writ teaches that the Christian Referendum is God's intuition of a person's free will to choose HIM. Apostle Peter's statement in 1 Peter 1: 2 is unambiguous. THE LORD selected Christians through His knowledge and the Holy Spirit's work so they can obey Jesus Christ.

The ALMIGHTY CREATOR'S aspiration is that a person should decide for righteousness. However, everybody has a choice to accept Him as the Supreme Being. And Him being the Author of Our Salvation has made it possible to reconcile with Him through His SON's shed Blood. However, the Creator does not override an individual's free will to choose Him.

Still, in His foresight, he knows who will pick Him; therefore, HE elects and predestines them to match his purpose. The Apostle Peter also tells us that the Almighty is "not wanting anyone to perish, but everyone to come to repentance" (2 Peter 3: 9). But Jesus answered, "For wide is the door and broad is the pathway that leads to destruction, and many enter through it. But small is the port and narrow the highway that leads to life, and only a few can find it" (Matthew 7: 13-14).

Predestination is a hot topic of debate, according to R. C. Sproul. Saints get confused by complex discussions on Christian Election, Predetermination, and free will. The opposite faith uses its suppositional dogma list to contrast the opposing views. Then, they wrote volumes of books, frequently quoting Scriptures out of context to prove their doctrine was correct.

Usually, the winner is the denomination with the most massive information and the loudest voice. Yet, their victory gets them no closer to the correct interpretation in the light of the surrounding verses. However, the followers of Christ who lose face do not disappear into the darkness.

Instead, they point the finger of outrage at the brotherhoods who disagree with them and characterize them as icon-worshipers. In another chapter, we will process the exact interpretation of Sacred Writings. But if anyone thinks they could make the Bible mean whatever they want, it would not be much of a source of spiritual guidance.

Discussion of Christian Election stokes potent emotions. It is strange how the Glorified agrees on what color to paint the walls in a worship center. But they get lost in the conversation about salvation for a proportion and not others. So, they quote the Word texts out of context to conscript it as a pretext in two ways.

1. They forcefully scrutinized certain Scriptures as outliers to support their fallacious position.
2. They will soft pedestal the intent to defend their denominational dogma.

The Saints, who vaguely understand Election, their natural man, try to shout down the voice of genuine reason. To justify the erroneous information in their minds, to trust the thoughts of self-deception. The power of God is available to humankind to show salvation delivered and preserved by the undeserved favor of grace alone by faith.

An excellent example of Scripture's misinterpretation is (Mark 16: 17-18). "And these signs accompany those who believe in MY NAME: They shall cast out demons; speak in new tongues, collect serpents with their hands. If an individual drinks any deadly poison, it cannot damage them. And, the Saints who touch and agree on healing, the ill recover. However, one remembers that the prerogative of life or death belongs to God. So, the writer's point is this: a good rule to follow in context application is to ask yourself who is speaking and why.

Then, list all the information about the author. Where did the writing occur? Who are the principal characters to research in this verse? Who is their audience, and what is the global theme of the text? For instance, In this passage, The Good Shepherd gives "instructions to His disciples" before returning to God the Father. Jesus commanded His followers to preach and teach the Truth, no matter the cost. Preaching the Gospel is "the voice of honest people," or "excellent news" is the blessing that the Supreme Being who created all things will give unto the world.

Although Christian Election, Predestination, and Freewill relate to Understanding God's Character, Christianity is unassisted. The three doctrinal concepts become divisive when taken out of context but do not affect salvation. Contrariwise, they, together conceptually, generate confusion without assessing the theological meaning.

Believers often try to avoid debating God's character of choice. So, truth-seekers stay clear of Biblical squabbles to avoid religious confrontations. A lack of Godly wisdom causes misunderstanding and chaos among denominations. Every believer knows that "Jehovah is not the God of disorder, but peace, as in all the congregations of the Saints" 1 Corinthians 14: 33.

The Bible discusses the concepts of Election, Predestination, and free will. Together, they are challenging to understand. In addition, clarity is difficult to express or receive when an individual has an uncooperative mindset.

Let us simplify the subjects since the doctrines do not connect the theological elements. Free them from partisan influence and religious dogma. Then, the writer shall define them by contextualizing each word through the lenses of the Holy Spirit.

Biblical Predestination Defined: is an act of God whereby, in eternity past, THE LORD has chosen the people HE would save. Again, it is essential to note salvation is unconditional and does not count on anything outside of the All-Merciful plan for humanity. The Lord shows mercy to whom He wills. So, righteous preordination depends not on humankind's desire or efforts but on God's grace and forgiveness alone. God is merciful to millions and hardens the hearts of others who refuse to listen to Him (Romans 9: 18).

THE LORD says to Pharaoh: "I raised you for this very purpose, that I might display MY POWER in you and that everyone proclaims MY NAME in all the earth," study Romans 9: 15–17. So, the doctrine of Christian Predetermination is a command of the Almighty, which the Apostles, at length, taught in the New Testament.

The Biblical evidence of how God chooses

Paul the Apostle, writing to the Church at Ephesus, says preceding salvation, humankind was dead religiously in sin, Ephesians 2: 1-3. His message to Ephesus means: Deceased spiritually or incapable of responding to the Gospel without the Holy Purpose. Because flesh gives birth to satisfy the sinful nature, the Breath of God emanates holiness to meet the needs of the mortal soul.

Jesus, speaking to Nicodemus about rebirth, said, "born of water" refers to the physical birth; He refers to the woman's sac that holds amniotic (fluid), the first birth. The second is "the Spirit," which guides the Christians' spiritual birth. Thus, believers are born twice, or "water and spirit."

Sinners cannot respond to salvation without Jehovah's Presence. Hence, they cannot love Christ the Lord, accept His Commandment, or satisfy Him. Unbelievers' thoughts oppose the Savior and do not align with His Law because the fleshly heart cannot make the Supreme Being happy. (Romans 8: 7-8).

THE LORD must take the first steps in Electing Christians. Again, no sinner could save her or himself from eternal cessation. The doctrine of Election is why the Messiah said in John 6: 44, "No one shall come to Me unless the Father who sent Me draws him." Our Lord's Bible emphasizes that salvation is the work of The Maker of Heaven and Earth. The Prince of Peace shows humankind's inability to save themselves spiritually. Note the Holy Writ below will likewise show Emmanuel's Hand in the Biblical Election:

For the Lord has commanded this of us: "I have made you a light for the Gentiles, that you may bring salvation to the ends of the earth" Acts 13: 47 (NIV84).

For instance, the Apostle was preaching to a crowd in Macedonian. Like the above, one lady listening was Lydia, a dealer in purple cloth from Thyatira, who was a worshiper of the King of Kings. Jesus Christ opened Lydia's mind to respond to Paul's message (Acts 16: 14).

The Alpha and Omega could only open their hearts to receiving the Gospel (of Election) to heed what Paul spoke. The Holy Bible points us to a critical truth that is uplifting and awe-inspiring simultaneously: ONLY the Messiah can do THE CHOOSING AND SAVING! Sacred Scripture shows CHRIST THE LORD does the redeeming; His sovereign Hand is at work in the Sacred Text of Acts chapter 16.

Not to be redundant, but it was THE LORD WHO opened the heart of Lydia and not only every believer to receive HIS Gospel teachings. Still, THE Humble Spirit moves to prove the pure essence of the Biblical Election. Starting the Divine Meaning of SPIRITUAL TRUTH is vital for human salvation. Often, the human flesh wants to decide the path and demands the Paraclete to follow us. Look, THE INTERCESSOR does not move in the direction we choose for Him. He is like the river, and we must flow with Him.

Only the Supreme Goodness can show how His perfect righteousness will justify the guilty sinner. Still, the Maker of Heaven and Earth wants His Elected supporters to understand the Gospel, believe in it, preach it to us, and then proclaim it to a lost world.

Jehovah searches the heart and brings conviction for transgressions. The Saints must be conscious. The Author of all things solely leads the trespasser to the truth about redemption. It is why THE LORD in the Body of Jesus died on the cross for humanity's evil act and rose again from the dead. So, only HIS Humble Spirit could lead wrongdoers to take the first steps of salvation. "For he chose us in him before the world's creation to be pure and blameless in his sight."

Biblical Predestination and Free Will

"For those God foreknew, He also predestined to be conformed to the likeness of his Son, that he might be the firstborn among many brothers. And those he predetermines, Jesus likewise announced those HE called HE also sustained," and THE LORD said this: "When I justify, I still Glorify." Romans 8: 29–30.

The theological definition of predestination is that the LORD bequeathed all occurrences; therefore, all circumstances are contingent on the predetermined events of humankind's souls. Ephesians 1:5 states that God predestined us to be His sons through Jesus Christ.

Predestination is a conversion matter rather than a justification concern—study Romans chapter Eight. The Christian decision defines free will to worship without worrying about our shortcomings. Despite this, there are various opinions on the doctrine of Christian volition, making it hard for Christians to learn.

They find it challenging to separate God's control from human freedom of choice and how they interrelate. Determinism and fatalism can confuse anyone, suggesting no control. But the doctrine of salvation is absolute because of the eternal decree of God.

Believers can trust the Word of God for help, but going alone is a disaster. The scriptures help Saints make wise choices about Predestination and free will.

1. "Before I formed you... I knew you before you were born. I separated you; I appointed you as a prophet to the nations." Jeremiah 1: 5.
2. "No, we speak of Almighty's secret wisdom, a hidden pearl of knowledge, and Jehovah destined for our glory before time began," 1 Corinthians 2: 7.
3. When God, who set me apart from birth and called me by his grace, was pleased. Galatians 1:15 (NIV84).
4. For he chose us in him before the world's creation to be holy and blameless in his sight, in Love. Ephesians: chapter 4 (NIV84).
5. He told us the mystery of his will according to his good pleasure, which he purposed in Christ. Ephesians 1: 9 (NIV84).

Saints benefit from salvation in Jesus Christ. They also show that the Alpha and Omega predetermined the righteous; certain people are the unique exceptions. "For God so loved the world that he gave his one and only Son, that whoever believes in him shall not perish but have everlasting life." John 3: 16 (NIV84).

Predestination comprises two words: "Pre," meaning "before," and "destination," showing the final induction. The Saints' journey is to determine (Predestined) where they will go after they leave the earth.

For example, the writer ordered a package not in stock earlier this year. He left his information on where to send his product when it arrived. He foreordained his parcel to travel from the store to his home, the last destination. The box could have been anywhere if I had not given it a pre-forwarding address.

Individuals accept Jesus Christ as Lord and Savior, allowing them to enter the Kingdom of Glory after death. Predestination tackles the paradox of free will and the unknown factors in soul salvation. Rejecting the Good Shepherd means no eternity; God's wrath remains. John 3: 36 (NIV84).

Listen, God is not an evil, sadistic monster. He is Love and created individuals for His good pleasure. His taking pleasure in those with no choice but to reject Christ is confusing. That being so, Scripture will prove that God's discrimination in His relations with humans is both righteous and sovereign.

Yet, THE LORD speaks tough Love when He inherently chooses souls for eternal salvation and passes over another. Regardless, THE LORD'S rejection of others and acceptance of an unspecified is the Achilles' heel of the study of predestination. That is the reason a multitude has deemed foreordination unfair.

The Almighty agrees with HIS Word's fundamental moral or ethical code; the disciples are preferential. He chose us in him before the world's creation to be holy and blameless in his sight. In Love, THE SUPREME CREATOR predestined and adopted Christians as HIS children through Jesus Christ, re his pleasure and choice, Ephesians 1: 4–5. However, HE refuses others because they do not acknowledge the principles of The Prime Mover. Instead, they live to satisfy their sinful practices.

The people HE refuses are unbelievers, the vile, the murderers, the sexually immoral, those who practice magic arts, the idolaters, and all liars. As per the scripture of Revelation 21: 8, they shall live in the fiery lake of burning sulfur. Listen, those who oppose the Gospel accept man's wisdom, not God. 1 Thessalonians 4: 8. Then THE LORD rejects them.

Jesus said, "Not everyone who calls me 'Lord' will enter the kingdom of heaven, only those who do the will of my Father." On that day, many may say, "Jesus, did we not prophesy in YOUR NAME and drive out demons and perform a profusion of miracles? Then I will tell them, I never knew you, away from ME, you evildoers." Matthew 7: 21–23.

The Maker of Heaven and Earth predestined humankind to act without authoritative constraints. However, the human parents initially failed to keep a specific commandment. We needed eternal restoration to help humans choose rightly.

So, the Divine Father preeminently preordained humanity's salvation by giving THE NAZARENE. It is the reason Jehovah said, "He would put enmity between Satan and the woman, and between His offspring and hers; he shall crush your head, and you would strike his heel." Genesis 3: 15 (NIV84). Note this is about Predestination and free will. The ALMIGHTY is not answerable to humanity. However, HE is dependable to act coherently with His Holy Character, as seen in the righteousness of His Son, Jesus Christ.

Still, there are legitimate questions to answer. What happens to free will if the Maker of the Universe and Earth already preordained humankind? Are humans mere dolls on a string, doing what the Supernatural Deity ordained without a choice? Does the Infinite Spirit decree the individuals who should go to paradise in advance? If so, what is the reason for evangelism? Why witness if THE LORD has preordained salvation? How can those who sin be responsible if the All-Merciful - have predetermined certain people for eternal damnation?

Concededly, Christian Election, Predestination, and Freewill are complex doctrines. No declaration could explain the unique elements of the Father's sovereignty to humankind's accountability. We should adhere to the details revealed in Deuteronomy 29: 29. The Glorified explore Christian Eternity, Predetermination, and free will while upholding God's plan. Those the Supreme Being foreknew, HE "also predestined the Saints to reconcile to the likeness of his Son," Romans 8: 29. Hence, no one can dispute the fact is Biblical reality.

www.ingramcontent.com/pod-product-compliance
Lightning Source LLC
LaVergne TN
LVHW041623070526
838199LV00052B/3226